Henry the Stephenson House Mouse:
A Diary

Henry the Stephenson House Mouse: A Diary

By Karen Campe Mateyka

WITH ILLUSTRATIONS BY
KATHRYN STULLKEN HOPKINS

St. Louis, Missouri

Copyright © 2007, Reedy Press
All rights reserved

Reedy Press
PO Box 5131
St. Louis, MO 63139
USA

No part of this publication may be reproduced or transmitted in any form or by any means, electronic or mechanical, including photocopy, recording, or any information storage and retrieval system, without permission in writing from the publisher.

Permissions may be sought directly from Reedy Press at the above mailing address or via our website at www.reedypress.com.

Library of Congress Control Number: 2006940122

ISBN: 978-1-933370-07-1
1-933370-07-6

For all information on all Reedy Press publications visit our website at www.reedypress.com.

Printed in Canada
07 08 09 10 11   5 4 3 2 1

CONTENTS

Preface   *vii*

Acknowledgments   *xi*

The Diary   *1*

Henry's Tour of the Stephenson House   *151*

Stephenson Family Tree   *160*

Henry's Family Tree   *163*

PREFACE

In 1999, as a member of the Edwardsville Historic Preservation Commission, I watched the restoration of the Stephenson House begin and grow into a most fantastic project. I loved every minute of it! A restoration of this magnitude in Edwardsville was incredible and truly a once-in-a-lifetime experience for all of us.

The search for more history of Col. Benjamin Stephenson began as the restoration progressed and evidence of original windows, covered stairs, and an attached kitchen was found. After I had searched for about two years, asking questions, sending letters, reading good historical references, and conducting genealogical searches of Col. Ben, wife Lucy, and children Julia, James, Elvira, and Benjamin V., the story began to unfold.

The restoration, the family history, and genealogy discoveries caused excitement among members of the Historic Preservation Commission and the Friends of the Stephenson House. We all felt that we should share this treasure trove with our community. But how?

Henry was created and was characterized as the Stephenson House mouse—long-time resident of the Stephenson House. He loved old stories and remembered family stories passed down by the Stephenson House mouse relatives, one of which was great-great-great grandfather Samuel who came from Virginia with the Stephenson family.

Henry, the friendly, intelligent little mouse who loves corn chips, reaches out to the community through his bi-weekly column in the *Edwardsville Intelligencer*. He gave the readers current details about the restoration and encouraged folks to see the actual restoration at the numerous "Take-A-Peek" events. Through Henry, the community learned the historical information about Col. Ben and his family. It was Henry who knew birth dates, places where the Stephensons had lived, their friends and business partners, and how they arrived in Illinois. It was Henry who told us about the good things Col. Ben accomplished for the folks in the Illinois Territory when he was a delegate in the United States House of Representatives.

The stories that Henry "remembered" came in bits and pieces from West Virginia, Kentucky, Tennessee, California, Pennsylvania, Texas, New Jersey, and South Carolina, as well as from the Illinois Territory from towns such as Kaskaskia, Carlinville, Springfield, and Peoria. Ol' Henry's stories appear as the information came to me. They therefore do not necessarily or always appear in time order in the *Intelligencer*. I wrote what I learned, or what occurred, as soon as I knew about it.

More than one hundred Henry columns appeared in the *Intelligencer* devoted to Henry's best efforts to keep all ages informed on the progress of the restoration. He also reported on the genealogy and history of Col. Ben and his family and life in the early 1800s on the frontier in Edwardsville. As the information arrived from various sources, it began to complete the Stephenson history and the genealogy puzzle. In spring 2006, the Stephenson history and genealogy were considered complete — as reasonably as possible — and the restoration of the house was completed at the same time. A very good year!

It has been so much fun. I have learned so much, and I hope you have too. It was double fun for me from the very beginning when Henry's true identity was unknown. I do hope there are still some folks out there who are surprised!

Hey guys, I could not have written this if you had known who Henry was! And, for those of you who did know, I am glad you didn't tell me!

See ya' later,
Henry

ACKNOWLEDGMENTS

There are so many, many people who have helped and supported me as Henry grew into a mouse that needed lots of attention and information to keep him going! My family has been most supportive and patient when Henry became a household word. Each one had his niche. My husband Bill kept the commas in the right place. My daughter Sally ran the errands. My son Dan and wife Denise kept the computer running, while their daughter, Taylor, kept a secret. She did not tell anyone that her grandma was Henry!

Henry grew into an incredible mouse with a prodigious memory. His memory was possible because people from far and wide provided information, which enabled me to track the early history of Benjamin Stephenson and his wife Lucy Swearingen. There are so many to thank—too many to mention, I'm sure I'll forget someone.

Kathryn Stullken Hopkins sketched Henry in the very beginning. There he was, reading the *Spectator* with his little glasses perched on his nose! My friend Kathryn graciously contributed the illustrations for this book, and over the years she has added a lot of laughter to my life as Henry grew.

I offer my profound appreciation to Dr. Joseph Weber, who encouraged me as Henry developed into a mouse that loved school children. Joe was always available to help, just as he had advised and supported me over the years with various preservation efforts.

Kudos to Dr. Sidney Denny for his incredible and

unrelenting search through old newspapers and other documents in many history libraries. For this he has my deepest thanks and respect. His search has brought to light valuable and complete information about Col. Ben and his political, military, and business experiences in Illinois.

There are so many whose help was invaluable in the Stephenson search. Don Wood of the Berkeley County Historical Society pointed me in the right direction on the Stephenson search. Kathryn Harris of the Abraham Lincoln Presidential Library provided invaluable information that led to Columbia, Missouri, and Stephenson descendants. Judy Thompson of the Edwardsville Public Library located many resources used in the Stephenson search. The Kentucky Historical Society, the Brooke County Historical Society, Wellsburg, West Virginia, Shannon Berry of the Missouri Historical Society, and the State Historical Society of Missouri all searched their records when I needed answers.

Many thanks to Keith and Jack Whitener and E. J. Holly for patiently explaining about bricks, bricklaying, plastering, fences, kitchens, wood gutters, and beehive ovens!

Henry was created and existed due to the efforts of Edwardsville people. A very special thanks to retired Senator Evelyn Bowles, who secured state funds for the purchase and restoration of the Benjamin Stephenson House. The support of the City of Edwardsville, Norm Nilsson and the Madison County Sheriff's Work Alternative Program, and the many generous people in the great community of Edwardsville made the Stephenson House happen. Without them, Henry would never have been created! Once again, Edwardsville has shown it is a wonderful place to call home!

Come visit the 1820 Colonel Benjamin Stephenson House—you will enjoy it. And, who knows, you may spot Henry running around!

AN INTRODUCTION

January 9, 2002

Please allow me to introduce myself; I am Henry the resident mouse at the Stephenson House. I call myself the Stephenson House Mouse. I live at the Stephenson House at 409 S. Buchanan St. in Edwardsville, Illinois. I have lived here for many years, and I have heard and seen lots. I am also one of those unique individuals who love old stories that are passed down through the generations. There are family history stories about when Col. Benjamin and Lucy left Virginia in 1800. I have heard these stories from the descendants of great-great-great grandfather Samuel, the very first mouse that lived at Col. Ben and Lucy's. I even can recall the stories told about the parents of Col. Ben and Lucy's family. I love these old stories, and I love to reminisce about the old days. I want to talk about these events in the lives of the Stephensons, AND I want to tell you all about what is going on at the Stephenson House today! I have always thought the life of Col. Ben and Lucy was exciting, and it gave me lots to think about. WELL, what is happening at 409 S. Buchanan these days is one of the most exciting stories that I have seen or heard in a long, long time.

Christmas has just passed, and I have received a great gift—a new roof! Have you seen my house in the last few weeks? There are wreaths on the doors and candles in the windows just like in the old days and now a new roof. That roof was really needed; believe me, Henry the old mouse who lives here knows. Did you know that the new roof is just like the one Col. Ben had put on in 1820? I know, because I was here the day E. J. and Keith, the carpenters, found an old shake shingle in the attic that was from the 1820 roof. They found a guy who could make shingles just like the ones from 1820; they are called double sawn shingles. The roof that is on the Stephenson House today is made of shingles just like the ones from 1820. Now, that is called restoration!

There have been various people living in this house over the years. Some I have known and others I know about from family stories. The last people who lived here were a group of boys who were here a long time. Then about two years ago, the boys moved out, and I hid outside. I did not want to be in the wrong box and be moved away from here. Next thing you know, the boys were gone and there were all kinds of people tearing things up around here! I am a small mouse and was quite scared. Those people tore down the old porch, took the plaster off the walls, and even took the boys' bathroom out. When they took out the radiators I was really worried—how would I keep warm all winter?

I am an old mouse, and I have heard many stories about Col. Ben and Lucy building this house and how they put their heart and souls into the planning and building. I was really upset when I saw all the tearing up going on around here.

Then one day, I heard Jack and Laura, they are the restoration architects, talking to a fellow named Joe, and I started to feel better. They were talking about fixing this house up to be just like it was when Col. Ben and Lucy and the kids lived here! Joe was here later with his friend Jim, and they were taking down the door frames, doors, and mantels that Col. Ben had his carpenters make many, many years ago. Joe and Jim talked about the Edwardsville Historic Preservation Commission, who is in charge of restoring the house.

I learned that restoring a house means to put the building back just like it was when it was built by using as much of the original as possible as well as authentic reproductions. Joe and Jim, who are from HPC, were grinding the nails down in the woodwork and putting little numbered gold tags on each piece so they would know which room it came from. What a job!!! I listened to them talk a long time, and I knew it was going to be OK. HPC members and Neil, Joe's son, even raked the leaves one day—now, I really had to stay out of their way!! I don't know who HPC is but they sure care and are spending a lot of time working around here.

Sandy and Andrew were helping one day, and it sounds like they are part of a group called the Friends of the Col. Benjamin Stephenson House. These people are trying to find ways to raise money to restore the house and ways to tell the people of the area about the house and Col. Ben. I heard them say that if you want to help you just talk to Carol Wetzel who is president of that group.

Well, these folks are around a lot these days, and I feel at home with them. I know Col. Ben and Lucy would be pleased. They were married almost twenty years before they built this house. They were so happy and had parties and lots of fun with their friends, and the kids loved this place. Poor Col. Ben died after living in this house for just ten months. There were a lot of tears shed by Miss Lucy and the children when he passed. The story that comes down through the Stephenson House mouse stories is that Lucy and the younger kids stayed in the house for twelve years after Col. Ben's death. The youngest daughter, Elvira, got married to Bill Starr and went to Carlinville, young Ben went to Galena, and Lucy finally went to Carlinville to be with her family.

When I look back over the last couple years, I know Col. Ben and Lucy would be really proud of what is occurring at their house. Ol' Henry here has been thinking and there are a lot of Stephenson House mouse stories about Col. Ben and his family that I am remembering. I will be back to keep you up-to-date on the progress of the house restoration, AND I will give you lots of information on the Stephenson family.

    See ya' later,
    Henry

REDISCOVERING THE 1820s

January 16, 2002

Hi! Henry, the Stephenson House Mouse, is back. Things are really moving around my house! E. J., Keith, and Greg, the guys who do the restoration work from St. Louis Tuckpointing and Painting, are doing a lot with bricks!! I'll tell you about that in a minute.

The other day, I found a big piece of hotdog bun in the front yard that somebody at Dairy Queen dropped—it sure was good! As I sat there eating and looking at the house, I got to remembering some of the old stories about Ben's family. James Stephenson, Ben's dad, came from Ulster, Ireland, and married Mary Reed in York County, Pennsylvania, in 1763 where Ben and his brothers and sisters were born. Ben's dad was a private in the Pennsylvania Militia in the Revolutionary War.

After the war when Ben was about twenty years old, the Stephenson family moved to Martinsburg, Virginia. Ben and Lucy met in Brooke County, Virginia, and soon were married. Col. Ben and Lucy lived at Harpers Ferry when their daughter Julia was born in 1803, and four years later they moved on to Logan County, Kentucky. A few more years passed, and the family came to the Illinois Territory and the town of Kaskaskia. Great-great-great grandfather Samuel Mouse used to tell how he hid in different places in the wagon during the moves. Those were exciting trips for him!

We mice are small and have to be careful, but I do listen to Joe, Jack, and Laura when I can. Remember I told you about those people that came and did all the tearing up around here—took out the bathrooms, radiators, and all that? I heard they were people from the Madison County Sheriff's Work Alternative Program, or SWAP, who help out when they are needed. Way it sounded to me, the folks at HPC went to Norm at the SWAP program for help. Jack the architect decided what had to be removed, and the Sheriff's SWAP program got it done. I overheard Joe, Jack, and Laura say it was removing all the "stuff" like the plaster that allowed them to see what the house really looked like in 1820. They discovered a lot about how the house was built, even a second stairway. Then the Stephenson probate records were located at a state records depository. These records included an inventory of Col. Ben's household goods, which in turn told a lot about the Stephenson lifestyle. Now everybody was excited! There was so much information around that HPC, Jack, and Laura just knew they had to take this house back to like it was in the 1820s.

The more I listen, the more I learn, and with that talk about the 1820s, Ol' Henry here knew something big was up. This restoration thing that is being done to "my" house is really something. From what I hear, it is rare that an old, old house is restored back exactly the way it was. You folks should watch what goes on around here with this restoration. From all I hear, this is a once-in-a-lifetime event for Edwardsville. Don't miss it!

Now, let's get back to the work going on now. The frames and doors were tagged and put in storage where they are safe during the heavy construction work. Next, E. J. had the guys put scaffolding up to stabilize the house. Then he changed big iron beams around, opened up windows that had been bricked up, and fixed floor joists. My mouse family has told a lot of stories about the size of those termites that ate on those floor joists back in the middle of the 1800s!! They were really some big dudes with mighty big teeth to do all the damage they did! E. J. is pretty smart when it comes to this restoring. He's been doing it for over twenty years. He left the old floor joists in and put new boards around the old. Got a lot of extra strength in the floor, saved the old joists from the original house, and saved the old floor on the second floor. Good going, E. J.! This old mouse is learning some new words about restoration and construction, and it sure keeps my mind alert!

Then the brickwork started. E. J. and his guys took out the four old fireplaces and chimneys and made new ones. Now that was a job I really watched. The bricks in those old fireplaces had to be removed one brick at a time so that there wasn't damage to the bricks or the house. I heard the guys say it sure was lucky the place didn't burn down long ago—those chimneys and fireplaces were not built for safety. Made me think of Col. Ben's friend, Ninian Edwards, the fellow for whom our town is named. Maybe the fireplaces were the reason Ninian's house burned down—it was built the same time as the Stephenson House, and I would bet the houses were built very much alike.

When you come here, take a good look. You can see where the guys have opened up windows that had been closed with brick. And, you will see where they filled in a door on the north side of the house that had been made some years ago. The big event was when they took down the south entranceway that had been added. Keith used a mixture of old and new brick to fill in the area, and now the shape of the house is like it was after the addition in 1845. There is so much to tell—that new brick came from Richards Brick in Edwardsville, and it looks so much like the original brick that it is incredible!!! And, 1845—well, I will tell you all about that addition at another time, on my mouse honor, I will.

Anyway, Keith is one good bricklayer—and he doesn't even get dirty! He and Greg have really done a lot of beautiful work with these bricks. Talking about bricks made me remember the stories I heard about the bricks that are in this house. I will save that for next time—I hear hammering from inside, got to go see what is going on now!!

See ya,
Henry

THE HOUSE GETS SOME FRIENDS

January 24, 2002

Hi! Henry the Stephenson House Mouse is here again. I sure am glad it has been a mild winter because there was a shortage of warm places to curl up in the Stephenson House until Keith and Greg got the fireplaces rebuilt. Now the fireplaces work, and we have nice warm fires in them! Well, I said I would be back to tell you about the bricks, and I will. But, I want to tell you something else first.

I heard Mary, Donna, and Wilma Jene talking about an annual meeting of the Friends group. Now I had to really pay attention because this is real new to me. What I understood was that a lot of the people who belong to the Friends of the Col. Benjamin Stephenson House met last week at Rusty's for dinner and a meeting. Sounds like there was a good turnout with special guests Senator Evelyn Bowles and Mayor Gary Niebur having a good time. Joe Weber spoke to the Friends group about the progress in the restoration of Col. Ben's house and thanked them for their great support. He showed pictures (slides, I think they are called) of how the house looked long ago, and he had pictures of Keith working with the bricks and other changes that have been made to bring the house back to how it was in 1820. Someone said Kathy was there in a dress and bonnet like Lucy would have worn. Sure wish I could have seen all that—but from the Stephenson House to Rusty's is a far piece for a mouse.

It is really pretty neat that the Friends had their first annual meeting at Rusty's. Let Ol' Henry tell you why. Samuel, the great-great-great grandfather mouse from way, way back, told the story that Col. Ben had built a brick house in Edwardsville around 1818. I could not remember that story, but it rang a bell. When the meeting was at Rusty's I remembered! Ben's house was one of the first on North Main Street. It was right across from the first courthouse, and Bob Pogue's store was next door. Then I knew! Bob Pogue built his store just to the south of Ben's house. Today, Rusty's Restaurant is in Pogue's building, and Col. Ben's first house was right next door. Bet Col. Ben and Lucy knew what was going on last week in their old neighborhood!

I overheard Karen—she is the one who likes to look up old records—talking about Ben and Lucy's first house. She said she found where Ben bought two lots on Main Street in 1817 and that he also had bills for shingles, nails, timber shingles, and sheeting plank at Abraham Prickett's store dated July 15, 1818. Those bills had to be for Ben's first house. When Col. Ben moved out, the Bank of Edwardsville used his house. This is not the same Bank of Edwardsville that I hear Bob Wetzel talking about!!!

When Col. Ben built "my" house here at 409 South Buchanan, he watched the construction very carefully because he was going to build a mighty fine elegant home, and he wanted it to be done right. I heard there are records that show where Col. Ben had Bill Hopkins bring a man over to the brickyard at the house site and had him dig clay for the bricks for a shed in February 1821. Col. Ben paid Bill Hopkins $4.50 for four days digging clay for bricks. Bill Hopkins was also hired to haul brick bats, plank, sand, wood, and the clapboard he had made for the shed and to clean away ground for the brick kiln. In June, when the hauling was over, there was a bill for fifty cents for two quarts of whiskey for hired hands that put up the shed. Hmmmm, wonder if that was a day's pay or an incentive to keep working?? That is one story this mouse did not hear before!

It must have been Jess, Hark, and the children — Col. Ben's indentured servants — who made the bricks for the shed — just like they did for the house. Col. Ben did not have a lot of workers so he hired help to dig the clay that was needed for the bricks. Then his people had to build the kiln, use the brick forms to make the bricks, and then do the firing. Keith and Greg figure there are at least four hundred thousand bricks in Col. Ben's house. That kiln must have been fired twenty-four hours a day for a long time! Then they had to have bricks for the smokehouse, the kitchen, the shed, and for the floor around the back porch. Lucy, coming from a fine family in Martinsburg, Virginia, wanted bricks around the back porch so that people did not have to walk in mud and dust before they came into the house.

The other day, Keith found a couple of bricks used in a wall of the house different from the others. These bricks were real, real hard and real dark. I was there when he found them. Keith said they were from the kiln wall and had been baked over and over as new bricks were made in the kiln. Keith also said they used broken bricks and these hard, hard bricks in spaces where they were not noticeable. As long as it took to make bricks, those people did not waste a single one!

Ol' Henry here is having a great time. I was just a plain old boring everyday mouse — now all this excitement, new people to watch and listen to, and best of all I am thinking! I am remembering those stories I heard as a kid.

Hey, I am out of here—E. J. and the gang just came back with food and I am hungry. Maybe they brought some of that good summer sausage from Joe's.

See you later,
Henry

HOW THE COLONEL
BECAME A COLONEL

February 13, 2002

Hey guys, before updating you on the progress of "my" house, let Ol' Henry just say I sure am glad I kept adding more fluff and newspapers to my bed. It is cold in "my" house! And, I want to explain why I always refer to Col. Ben as a colonel. If you can believe it, he got the title while in Illinois and before Edwardsville was officially founded!

When Territorial Governor Ninian Edwards arrived in Kaskaskia in 1809, his first job was to reorganize the territorial government. This was when Col. Ben was appointed sheriff. Edwards's next move was to form military companies. Old great-great-great granddaddy Samuel said he understood the U.S. was not too friendly with Britain after the Revolutionary War. He said that the British had been seizing U.S. ships and firing on some of our vessels. Also, there were some unhappy Indians. The Potawatomi, Kickapoo, Sac, and the Fox Indian tribes were not happy with how the territorial governments were making treaties for exchange of land. These tribes were siding with the British, so the people in the Illinois Territory were fearful of an Indian attack. Old Samuel said there were a lot of unhappy people, and he figured that was why Edwards got the militia going as soon as he got to the Illinois Territory.

Now, the reason I talk about dates and all that school book stuff is because I want you to *think!!* It was not many years after the Revolutionary War that Col. Ben and Ninian Edwards came to Illinois. They came only five years after Lewis and Clark left Wood River in 1804 on their famous journey! Ol' Henry just wants you to have an idea of how long ago this all happened!! As you can see, it was long, long, long before Henry was born!

Old Samuel told of how Edwards appointed men from Kaskaskia and the surrounding area as captains of militia companies in St. Clair and Randolph Counties. The captains then appointed officers for their companies. In May 1809, they were preparing for war in the Illinois Territory. Edwards knew about the trouble with the Indians around Virginia and the Ohio River when that area was a new frontier. The mouse stories say Old Samuel said over and over that Edwards and his men wanted to be prepared for trouble.

Good thing Edwards prepared the Illinois Territory so well, because in 1812 war broke out with Britain and their Indian allies. Great-great-great granddaddy Samuel loved to tell stories about the war, and he educated all of us on the War of 1812. He talked about a trade ban imposed on Britain in 1810 but Britain refused to cooperate. Finally, President James Madison had had enough, so he called Congress into session in November 1811 to prepare for war. War was declared on Great Britain on June 18, 1812. Old Samuel told how Col. Ben was right there defending the Illinois Territory, serving in two campaigns of that war. Funny thing though, Old Samuel never talked about his being with Col. Ben in the war! I believe he stayed home!

Elizabeth of HPC found records that show Ben was elected brigade inspector, brigade major, and then appointed adjutant general. I heard her explain that the adjutant general helped Commander-in-Chief Edwards by sending out orders, keeping records, and writing letters. Guess you would say that Ben was Edwards's right-hand man. I also heard Elizabeth talk about Illinois records that show that on September 12, 1812, troops under the command of Maj. Benjamin Stephenson were at Fort Russell. He was in command of eight companies with a total of 570 men. I think you all know that Fort Russell was somewhere just north of Edwardsville. It must have been a big fort! By the end of the War of 1812, Benjamin Stephenson had received the title of colonel.

Col. Ben served as sheriff of Randolph County from 1809 until 1813, when he was appointed to serve as a delegate to Congress from the Illinois Territory. He served in the House of Representatives in 1814 and 1815, at the same time James Madison, the man our county is named for, was president. Remember, it took thirty-five days to get to Washington, D.C., from Kaskaskia. Just think how much Ben must have cared about the future of the Illinois Territory and its people!

Let's get back to "my" house and see what is going on! I was talking about the great breezes that come in these windows. When the people from SWAP were removing the plaster, they uncovered brickwork that helped the architects know what kind of windows had been at the top of the stairs. It was easy to see that the window at the back of the stairs had been filled in. This space has been opened and a replacement window is ready.

The window in front was the big, big surprise! This window had been made smaller! It was originally a Palladian window. The best Ol' Henry could understand from the talk around here was that a Palladian window is wider than the usual window and has a fan-shaped window at the top of it. E. J. and his guys are making a Palladian window, and soon the breeze will blow through on the stairs from front to back of the house. The breezes will blow like great-great granddaddy Ezra remembered. These replacement windows even have one-hundred-year-old glass in them! It seems that E. J. can find the best stuff for the best prices!!!

Now let me tell you about the heat from the fireplaces. Some of the owners have made changes to the house over the years. The Frank Dickmann family owned the house in the early 1900s. Yes, you are right. Ben Dickmann, our former police chief, is related to the family! At that time, Victorian homes were all the rage, and the Dickmann family wanted a fashionable house so they made some Victorian changes. One change was to make the downstairs doorways wider. When HPC decided to restore the house back to the 1820s, those doorways had to be restored to the original size. Keith found the original doorway size, and he added brick to make the opening smaller. The size of those doorways sure makes a difference in heating. Carol and Donna will tell you that when those fireplaces are going, this house is warm!

"My" house just feels good! I spend a lot of time thinking about the 1820s, Ben and his family, and all that went on here. HPC and the Friends of the Stephenson House are making plans for you to come here this spring. Be sure to stop by, I know you will like "my" house.

See ya' later,
Henry

SECURING THE FOUNDATION WITH A FRIENDS' AUCTION

March 20, 2002

You know it has been so quiet around here that I finally got used to it. Then one day people came in like a whirlwind, and things livened up. There were a whole bunch of people here, and they were talking about the 50/50 Auction, which will be held on May 18 on the lawn of "my" house. What I understand is that the Friends of the Benjamin Stephenson House need people to donate items for the auction. Then the item is auctioned off, and half of the money received will go to the donor and half to the Friends of the Stephenson House. That is why it is called a 50/50 Auction. Ol' Henry wants to remind the donors that they can choose to give their half of the proceeds to the Stephenson House to help with the restoration costs!

I listened real careful and learned that Jim Zupanci is in charge of this auction. Jim says he needs quality items for the auction, but they really don't have to be old. He said he would even take Waterford and Hummels (now those are words I do not understand), and he talked about old books, duck decoys, pianos, and paintings—either prints or rare paintings like a Van Gogh would do just fine. Jim said just no old refrigerators or recliners, and then he laughed. Henry thinks Jim is fun! Then Jim said that Gary Niemeier and Gerald Ahrens will be the auctioneers and will donate their time to the Stephenson House.

Well, I think it is about time I told you what brought Col. Ben to Edwardsville. The reason Col. Ben came to Edwardsville is because President James Madison appointed him receiver of moneys of the Land Grant Office on April 16, 1816. He did not return as U.S. congressman; instead, he came here for his new job. John McKee, who later became Ben's good friend and business partner, was appointed register of the Land Grant Office.

Now, just what was that Land Grant Office? Deanna said the federal government had finished surveying all the land north of Kaskaskia in the Illinois Territory, and it was now for sale. The Land Grant Office was established to handle the sale of this land. Remember, the Illinois Territory went all the way up to the Canadian border and included upper parts of Michigan, all of Wisconsin, and the part of Minnesota that is east of the Mississippi River. It is pretty good for an old mouse to remember all that, right? So, Col. Ben and John McKee were in charge of the sales for all those people who came to Edwardsville to buy land in the Illinois Territory. Talk about a big job! Can you imagine all the people that came to Edwardsville to go to the Land Grant Office!

Amanda, the archivist, said Col. Ben bought two lots on North Main when he came to town. In December 1816, he bought Lot 6, which is just to the north of Lincoln School. In January 1817, he bought Lot 23, and Amanda says in the following September a record shows Col. Ben was residing in his house on Lot 23. Lot 23 was across from the jail and the courthouse in the Public Square. I hear HPC people talk, and now I finally know where that lot was. You all know the spot—it is at Rusty's Restaurant. Karen says Lot 23 is where the big dining room and dance floor are located. One of these days Henry here is going to journey down that way and take a look. I hear the food is good and ya' never know, Dale might make sure I get a few tidbits. Be worth the long trip!

Enough about Col. Ben's first house, let's talk about "my" house. I have to tell you about a scary thing that happened with the restoration here. Ever since I have been here there has been a big steel beam in each of the ceilings of the two rooms downstairs. They were not real pretty, but they did manage to keep the upstairs floors from falling down. When Jack and Laura, the architects, started on the plans I heard from the very start that the steel beams had to go. I kept thinking "go where?" and "what will happen to 'my' house?" E. J. knew how to do it, and believe Henry, I heard all the talk and I listened closely. E. J. had put up scaffolding to stabilize the house while the beams were moved and all the interior and exterior brickwork was being done. To tell you the truth, the day E. J. and the guys moved those beams I took a long walk. I just didn't want to see what could happen. Well, when I came back, the beams were down, the floors shored up, and the house still standing! Then the next thing E. J. did was to use those steel beams to reinforce the downstairs floors of the 1845 addition. I have to admit, I left that day too. Henry just could not watch those guys carry those beams into that little cellar and then squeeze into that tiny crawl space to put the beams in place. When I came back, they had it done and they were all smiling. Wow!

Next, they repaired the floor joists under the second floor. Remember I told you about those giant termites and all the meals they had on the original floor joists? Well, some of those joists had to be replaced as the termites had really done a job on them. Luckily, E. J. was able to use a lot of the 1820 joists sandwiched between new joists. Now we have a sturdy floor. There was a time when I could tell that the guys were being very careful about how many people were upstairs at one time. Things are looking good!

See ya' later,
Henry

WHEN COUSINS COME KNOCKING

April 11, 2002

Golly, have I been busy. I have had relatives visiting and big machinery outside. One day last week, all sorts of clanging and banging and loud motor sounds started over at the old Clark filling station lot. They were cleaning up the lot and tearing down the canopy where the pumps had been. Turns out it was the Keller boys, Dale and Jim, helping out the Friends of the Benjamin Stephenson House. It was one of those big projects that a wise mouse stays away from, so I watched from inside "my" house. The lot sure looks good now, and I bet it will be used during the 50/50 Auction in May.

Henry here sure hopes that a lot of you donate stuff to the auction because I just know the Friends of the colonel need to earn lots of money. You know a mouse isn't too concerned about money, but it did come to my little mind when the Kellers were working on the Clark station lot. I suddenly realized that the Friends had to pay a lot of money for that land. They really need the space for parking, gardens, and small outbuildings, and I'm thinking they had to go to Bob's bank and borrow money. Now, from what I understand, when you borrow money you have to pay money back to the bank each month.

So, all this noise that is going on next door is causing me to get a little jumpy, especially when I heard a knock at my door late one afternoon. I opened the door and who appears but Cousin Zack from Kaskaskia! I hadn't heard from him in so long I was beginning to think he had run into one of those traps. He came to tell me what he had been able to find out about life in Kaskaskia when Ben and Lucy were there. I showed him around "my" house, and then we settled down with a bag of chips Cousin Zack had found.

Cousin Zack started telling stories. First, we talked about the big earthquake of 1811. It had really been felt in Kaskaskia, and we both wondered why we had never heard any stories about Ben and Lucy and the earthquake. Zack said Ben and Lucy and a lot of other families had settled in Prairie Du Rocher, which is near Kaskaskia. The people of the area were French and enjoyed a slow pace of life. They lived in houses built of stone, farmed, and loved music, dancing, games, and socializing. He said the Pierre Menard and Nathanial Pope mouse families still talk about the fun they had the first winter when the folks came from Kentucky to the Illinois Territory.

Cousin Zack told me what some of Ben's jobs were when he was sheriff of Randolph County. He said it was the sheriff who brought people into court for outstanding bills and had to collect the money. The sheriff also took the census of the county and collected the taxes, which included a tax on single men! Now, just what did they have against single men?

Then the very next day, Cousin Elijah from Lexington, Kentucky, shows up at my front door! Spring must be the time for my relatives to travel. Elijah brought news about Lucy and Ben in Kentucky. He said Lucy Swearingen Stephenson had inherited a lot of land from her father "Indian" Van. You know, the Virginia planters needed a lot of land because they wore out their land raising cotton, making it necessary to buy new land so they could plant more cotton. It only took three years of cotton to wear out a piece of land. Anyway, back to Lucy and her land. In 1806, Lucy sold the land in Brooke County, Virginia, that she had inherited from her father to John Connell for $3,000. Well, we three cousins sat back, ate some more chips, and thought things over. We decided that Ben and Lucy now had cash, and they were getting ready to head for the Illinois Territory.

Cousin Elijah told us what he knew about the settlement of the Illinois Territory. President Jefferson was planning for the settlement of the land east of the Mississippi. Stephenson, Edwards, and many other men who later came to Edwardsville waited in Kentucky for the territory to open. These men were chosen by Jefferson to govern the territory and prepare it for becoming a state when the population reached the size required by law to be a state. The men and their families had to prepare well in advance before heading west to the Illinois Territory.

Soon after my relatives went home, there was more news at "my" house. Jeff the surveyor brought Karen a map he had made. The map shows the 182 acres that made up the Stephenson property. Next thing you know, Karen is in her car getting ready to drive around to figure out where the boundaries of the land are today. Was I excited! I jumped in the car when she wasn't watching and went with her. I was finally going to see what my great-great grandfather Ezra talked about. Oh, did I have a good time! Later, I heard her tell Kathryn how to find the boundaries using the street names today. The property forms a rectangle. Starting at the corner around Dewey Street and Sheridan you go down Sheridan, turn right on Jefferson, and then draw an imaginary straight line that runs behind the Market Basket property, behind Cherry, Plum, and Quince Streets. Then go through Grandview where Buena Vista crosses the north end of Grandview Drive. This line continues to the American Legion and then goes north on the west side of the Woodland School (the old Junior High). At the end of the school playground, which is on a line with Georgia Street, you turn to the east and the property line goes through the school property, across West Street and over to just behind the "island" on Benton Street. Here, there is a small square area that was not part of the property. The property starts again up near the Madison County Shelter Care and runs just south of Schwarz Street until you are back around Dewey and Sheridan. It was fun taking that ride to find the boundaries—you might enjoy the drive too!

Henry has more news! The paint removal is going to start on "my" house soon, so be watching! Boy, do I have a lot going on around me!

See ya later,
Henry

THE STEPHENSON CHILDREN

June 20, 2002

Henry here knows it is time to start telling you about the Stephenson children. Remember, Col. Ben and Lucy had two girls, Julia and Elvira, and two boys, James W. and Benjamin V. Let's begin with the story of Julia and her family. Col. Ben and Lucy named their first child Elinor Julia when she was born on November 24, 1803, in Harper's Ferry, Virginia. Later, she was called Julia E. Stephenson. This information is on her tombstone, which was a lucky find. Believe me, we would never have known these kinds of facts from great-great grandpappy Ezra! He just wasn't into things like dates of birth. Julia spent her first years in Virginia, Kentucky, and Kaskaskia, and when she was twelve the family came to Edwardsville. That was in 1817. In July 1820, Julia married Palemon Winchester here in Edwardsville. Kathryn is positive they had a beautiful grand wedding in the house on North Main Street! Palemon was a lawyer, born in Baltimore in 1794, educated in Tennessee and came to Edwardsville about the same time as the Stephensons.

In 1830, Julia, Palemon, and their children left Edwardsville for the new town of Carlinville. Palemon and William Starr, Julia's brother-in-law, opened one of the town's first stores. Palemon was the first lawyer in Carlinville and later became a probate judge. Julia was active in church work, and her name is found, as is Lucy's, as an original member of the first Presbyterian Church in Carlinville.

Julia and Palemon Winchester had nine children. The first child, Lucy Ann, died at eleven months in 1822.

Their second daughter, Miriam, was followed by Sarah, Elvira, Ellen, Benjamin S., Laura, James, and Texanna, who was the last child. Texanna was born in 1845, died at age two, and is buried in the Carlinville City Cemetery.

Before Ol' Henry tells you about all those kids, let me tell you about Palemon's death. He died in April 1860, leaving his widow Julia and various grown children. Palemon had broken his leg when he fell from a doorstep in 1856 and thereafter was confined to his bed up to the time of his death at age sixty-five. A tombstone for Palemon cannot be located, but he is undoubtedly buried at Carlinville City Cemetery in the Stephenson-Winchester family plot. At the time of his death, his wife Julia and daughter Laura were his only family living in Carlinville. They left town shortly after his death, which may be the reason for the missing tombstone.

All right, now let me tell you what happened to these Winchester children:

- **Miriam Shelby** received her middle name in honor of Anthony Shelby, who was Palemon's law instructor. She married Nicholas Boise, a merchant and local politician who was fifteen years her senior. She died childless in 1854 at the age of thirty-one and is buried in Carlinville City Cemetery.
- **Sarah** is found on the 1850 census at the age of twenty-three. The following year she married Benjamin Brazzell in Calhoun County, which is her last record.
- **Elvira** married Milton Matthews in Macoupin County in May 1850, and she just seems to have disappeared.
- **Ellen,** the fourth child, married William W. Freeman in Carlinville. She died in 1865 at the age of thirty-five and is also buried in the Carlinville City Cemetery. Ellen and William Freeman had four children, Marion, Virginia, William H., and a son Edward who died at the age of one year.

- **Benjamin S.** Winchester married Brookey Ann Yowell on October 15, 1857 in Carlinville. This couple also seems to have disappeared.
- **Laura** is on the 1850 Carlinville census and was living with her grandmother Lucy. The next census shows her with her mother Julia in 1860. These are the only two times Laura is found in records. It appears that another Winchester disappeared.
- **James,** the youngest son, is on the 1850 Carlinville Census at the age of eight. Guess what? It appears he disappeared too.

Henry thinks this is getting pretty serious, with so many of the Winchesters disappearing. Amanda and Karen have spent a lot of time searching the records, and they would have come up with something if the information was available.

Here is the fun part! Do you all remember how excited Henry here was when my unknown Cousin Elzey from Missouri appeared at my door? Hey, he had brought information with him about Julia and her children Elvira, Benjamin S., and James! They had disappeared all right, but he knew they had gone to Columbia, Missouri. Now, who would have ever thought to look there? Cousin Elzey's information led Amanda and Karen to search in Boone County, Missouri. What they found combined with what Cousin Elzey knew has helped to find most of the missing Winchester children!!

Elvira Winchester and her husband Milton S. Matthews evidently left Carlinville shortly after their marriage and before their first child Elvira Marion was born in 1855 in Boone County, Missouri. This child was followed by Sarah V., Frances Susan, Laura A., Nicholas, Lucy S., and Milton S. From the records the girls found, Milton was a very successful carriage manufacturer and an avid temperance advocate. They found cemetery records showing Milton was buried in 1875 at the age of sixty, and his wife, Elvira, died two years later at the age of forty-nine. Their daughter, Sarah V., was buried in 1880 next to her parents in the Columbia Cemetery. Sarah was twenty-three at the time of death.

Benjamin S., a teamster, and his wife Brookey also moved to Boone County from Carlinville. They apparently had no children. Cousin Elzey thinks Benjamin S. worked with Milton in the carriage manufacturing business. Guess who lived in Boone County with Benjamin S. and Brookey in 1870? None other than his mother Julia Stephenson Winchester, Lucy's daughter, and Palemon's widow! Julia lived to be seventy-seven years old, dying in 1880. Benjamin S. died in 1899 at the age of sixty-seven, and in 1930, Brookey died at the ripe old age of ninety!! They are all buried in the Columbia Cemetery. Amanda and Karen also found James, the youngest child of Julia and Palemon, in the Columbia Cemetery records where he was buried in 1873 at the age of thirty-one.

Once again, the Stephenson mouse family came to the rescue! Cousin Elzey sure helped clear up some of the "disappearing" children" of the Winchesters. So, now we know that Julia and her children Benjamin S., Elvira, and James left Carlinville for Columbia, Missouri, in Boone County, where they lived and are all buried in the Columbia Cemetery. The only child still missing is Laura, and somebody will find her! Maybe one of my mouse relatives will be the one!

Gee, I am exhausted and I bet you are too. This took a long time to explain, but nine children is a lot to talk about. Take care!

See ya' later,
Henry

ELDEST SON JAMES W. STEPHENSON

July 8, 2002

OK guys, Henry is back and now let's learn about James William Stephenson, son of Col. Ben and Lucy. Their second child, a son, was born in Virginia in 1806 and named for the men in Ben's family. When James W. was ten years old, in 1816, he came from Kaskaskia to Edwardsville with his parents and grew up in their house on North Main Street.

James left Edwardsville for Galena, Jo Daviess County, when he was twenty-two years old. I heard Amanda say she had read that James "was a strikingly handsome man, with a personality that quickly won him many friends" and that within two years he was involved in Jo Daviess County politics.

Karen and Amanda have found a lot written about James. Ol' Henry sure is glad because James seemed to be on the move, and Henry has never heard of any mouse relatives in his area. Guess they couldn't keep up with him!! The girls learned that James participated in the Black Hawk War and was captain of the Stephenson Company. This was a group of mounted rangers that fought a lot of battles. The Battle at Apple River in northern Illinois is always connected with Capt. J. W. Stephenson. He described the skirmish himself in a letter that appeared in a local paper under the headline "ANOTHER BLOODY BATTLE CONDUCTED BY CAPT. J. W. STEPHENSON!" By the end of the Black Hawk War, he had attained the rank of lieutenant-colonel.

James knew many important politicians. Amanda

and Karen learned of letters from various politicians including a chatty letter in 1834 from Jefferson Davis. Stephenson was elected to the Illinois State Senate in 1834 and very soon sought an appointment to the Land Office in Galena.

In early December 1834, he made a trip to St. Louis and married Ellen Kyle, a merchant's daughter. The couple evidently spent time in Edwardsville and Vandalia and did not return to Galena until spring. During his absence from Galena, he received good-natured letters from friends that mentioned drinking, card playing, ice sleighing on the river, and kidding James about why he didn't get back to Galena. Amanda and Karen are really getting a kick out of these letters.

James was appointed receiver of lands at Galena and Chicago and took office when he returned to Galena in April 1835. The Stephensons enjoyed an elegant lifestyle. When James and his bride arrived in Galena they rented a home and purchased furniture, including mahogany dining tables and sideboards, fine linen, and other furniture. James also purchased a fine carriage for Ellen to use when she went calling. They drank champagne and the finest brandy at their parties, and Ellen kept up on the literary topics of the day and read such authors as Lord Byron. She was dancing through her kid slippers every few nights and would have to buy new ones. Although James W. joined her with vigor in the social life, he never rested from his political duties.

At the Democratic Convention in Vandalia in December 1837, Stephenson was nominated for governor. The campaign was just underway when the opposition accused Stephenson of defaulting to the federal government on his accounts as receiver of lands at Galena. The charges had something to do with Stephenson having to accept payment for land in paper that was discounted by the time the payment was sent to the secretary of the treasury. The newspapers were full of the accusations against Stephenson. However, personal slander was so much a part of every political campaign in those days that many listened with half an ear.

I heard Karen tell Amanda that Lucy wrote her son encouraging him to fight the battle. She reminded him to attend to his health and to remember that all great men have enemies. Henry thinks this is another instance of Miss Lucy being the strong matriarch of the Stephenson family.

James was not a well man, and his friends repeatedly encouraged him to withdraw and rest from his strenuous life. Finally, his strength was not equal to fight the newspaper campaign. In the spring of 1838, he withdrew from the contest for governor, and Thomas Carlin was named in his place. James died less than one week after Carlin was elected governor in August 1838. He died of tuberculosis at his home in Galena at the age of thirty-two. He was buried the same day with military honors.

James left his widow, Ellen Kyle Stephenson with two small children, Kyle and Lucy. Did you notice the names of the children? Their son Kyle was given his mother's maiden name, and the little girl was named for her grandmother Stephenson. They kept the names in the family during those years! One-year-old Lucy died in 1838, the same year as her father. Ellen soon moved to Freeport with her three-year-old son Kyle and lived with her sister Jane Clark and her husband. Ellen married again in 1843 to Colonel William Mitchell of Freeport. She died of tuberculosis nine months after her second marriage, when she was only twenty-nine years old.

Jane Clark took Kyle into her own family, and when her husband was appointed surveyor general of New Mexico, Kyle moved west with the family. He died in Arkansas in 1864. Before Kyle's death he had his father's remains moved to the cemetery in Freeport where his mother and little sister were buried, and he erected a monument to their memory.

Well, I have talked enough and I am out of here. It is a very warm day and I am heading for Annie's Custard. I just know some little boy or girl will drop ice cream on their way home and I will be ready!

    See ya' later,
    Henry

ELVIRA AMANDA STEPHENSON

July 18, 2002

Today Ol' Henry is going to tell you about Elvira Amanda Stephenson, the third child of Col. Ben and Lucy. Elvira was born in 1809 in Logan County, Kentucky, and the family came to Kaskaskia when she was an infant. When Elvira was seven years old the Stephenson family moved to Edwardsville. Elvira grew up in Edwardsville when the town was aglow with social, political, and cultural activities. She was seventeen years old when the Kaskaskia newspaper announced her marriage to William E. Starr of St. Louis on April 26, 1827. They were married in Edwardsville by Thomas Lippincott, a justice of the peace who was also a Presbyterian minister. Ol' Henry did not know much more about Elvira until Cousin Seth from Carlinville stopped by for a visit. I asked lots of questions and got some answers from him about Elvira and William E. Starr and their family. Cousin Seth, though, didn't have all the answers. It turns out that some people can seem to just disappear from public record. Elvira and her first husband William, it turns out, were two of these people. Cousin Seth and Ol' Henry were happy when Elizabeth and Karen decided to dig deeper to track down Elvira and William. Thanks to some excellent leads from Sheila, Karen was able to find obituaries for Elvira and William, which answered many questions Cousin Seth and Ol' Henry had.

William died in Edwardsville at the age of forty-three on April 20, 1843. The obituary, found in the *Alton Telegraph and Democratic Review*, told that in 1818

Starr arrived in Edwardsville from Rome, New York, probably with his brother Henry Starr, and they both settled in Edwardsville. Henry soon moved to Alton. William served in the Black Hawk War and was justice of the peace and clerk of Madison County. In 1837, he was a member of the Illinois State Militia as aid de camp to the brigadier general of the 3rd division. The obituary stated that William left "a young and interesting family to mourn." He was described as a man endeared to others by his kind, gentle disposition and his ability to resolve differences.

Elvira, thirty-four at the time of William's death, was now a widow residing in Edwardsville with her four children, all under the age of twelve. The rest of her family lived in Carlinville. By 1850, Elvira appeared on the census of Carlinville, living with her mother Lucy.

Elvira died November 6, 1881, and her obituary was published in the *Carlinville Democrat*. Henry has to chuckle a little because Cousin Seth, who is from Carlinville and who knows everything, did not know that Elvira lived and died in Carlinville! The obituary was signed "WWF" and Karen knew immediately that this was William W. Freeman, who had married Ellen Winchester, daughter of Palemon and Julia Stephenson Winchester. Julia was the first Stephenson child and Elvira's older sister. Freeman had been a member of the Stephenson family for the thirty years since his marriage to Ellen Winchester in 1853. He knew the family story quite well, and in writing Elvira's obituary, he provided a wealth of information about the Stephenson family for future generations, including Elvira's birth date!

William W. Freeman wrote in Elvira's obituary that she was born in Kentucky on March 23, 1809. He wrote that Elvira and William E. Starr had four children, only one of whom survived her, a son, William H. Starr of the Territory of Arizona.

These two sentences gave researchers the correct answers to several questions. Freeman gave Elvira's actual birth date, which is the first time an actual date and year have been located. Elvira's year of birth had previously been a calculated guess from very early census records that did not show actual year of birth. The scant census information made it appear that both Elvira and Benjamin V. were born in 1812, which just did not seem correct. This mouse thinks that the researchers are now confident that Elvira was born in 1809 and Benjamin V. in 1812, as he stated on pension papers.

Elvira's age has always been a bit of a question. You might recall that the Carlinville Census of 1850 shows Elvira's age as thirty-eight. Well, the obituary information would make her age forty-one in 1850. Henry here says, "with a twinkle in my eye" that he suspects Elvira was "a courtin'" and lowered her age! Sure enough, the obituary tells that in 1851 she married thirty-year-old Enoch Wall, Macoupin County Clerk. Unfortunately, Enoch died in 1858.

In 1860, Elvira married for the third time, becoming the wife of William Maddox, a fifty-four-year-old farmer. Maddox died in early 1881, and Elvira died the same year at age seventy-two. Elvira is buried in her own lot in Carlinville Cemetery. Ol' Henry thinks Freeman is making a point when he says that Elvira was buried in her own lot in the Carlinville City Cemetery.

William W. Freeman knew so much about the family and preserved a lot of the family history in Elvira's obituary. He wrote that Elvira had remarkable experience and had passed through almost all the changes of fortune in her life. He tells of a fulfilled youth when Elvira was "reared amid wealth and fashion, she became one of the gayest of the gay, a belle among one of the first families of the Territory of Illinois." But, fickle fortune had reduced Elvira to "circumstances to the extreme of bitter poverty." Freeman writes that Elvira, who was called Auntie Maddox, had a kindly disposition, ready to lend a helping hand to the destitute and the afflicted. She looked on the bright side of life even though "she realized its bitterness and disappointments in many ways."

Freeman obviously felt tremendous pride for the Stephenson family and Elvira when he wrote, "She was among the last of the early settlers of Illinois, and particularly of Edwardsville, Madison County. She was the friend and associate of EDWARDS, WHITESIDES, PRICKETTS and others of the long ago."

Elvira's obituary has provided the researchers with dates, places, names of some of the Stephenson family friends, and more on the family's life style. Sadly, it is now known that Elvira, the gayest of the gay, reared in wealth and fashion, left this world in extreme and bitter poverty. Well, Henry here feels sad for Elvira. It has been a long search to find out about her life; now we know, and the search is ended.

Enough of the Stephenson family stuff! Ol' Henry is on his way across the street to find some of those sunflower seeds they eat during the ballgames at the Leclaire ball diamond. Wow, are they good!

See ya' later,
Henry

BENJAMIN V. STEPHENSON AND LIFE IN THE 1820s

July 31, 2002

I have been having some quiet times at "my" house lately. No workers and no guests, just very quiet. The other day I was sitting in the shade across the street just looking at "my" beautiful house and got goose bumps realizing all the fantastic things that have occurred here in the last year or so. Just incredible!!! Then I got a little teary eyed thinking about life when Col. Ben and the family lived here in 1820.

Ya' know, this place was far from town and quite self-sufficient. Great-great-great grandfather Samuel used to talk about orchards, vegetable and herb gardens, corn, potatoes, beef, and hogs that Col. Ben raised on his land. The hogs provided food, bristles, bones, hides, and fat for many very important household purposes. About the only food Old Samuel said Lucy bought was sugar, vinegar, and the spices they couldn't raise like nutmeg, cloves, and cream of tartar. He also said they shopped at Bob Pogue's store to buy indigo and yellow bark to dye fabric.

The year Col. Ben passed away, he and Lucy bought butter, corn, oats, potatoes, cornmeal, and flour. They paid $6.75 for twenty bushels of apples from their old friends John and Mary Robinson earlier that year. Old Samuel said he guessed Col. Ben wasn't feeling too well, and they were forced to buy some food that they usually raised themselves.

Of course, you must remember Col. Ben and Lucy loved to entertain, which means that at times they bought very fine items from Bob Pogue's store. One time they bought fifteen mackerel, a turkey, peppermints, bottles of wine, and cordials. Henry thinks they were getting ready for a pretty good party!

Well my friends, we are down to talking about Benjamin V. Stephenson, the last child born to Col. Ben and Lucy. Ol' Henry thinks the V. is for Van, Lucy's father's name! Benjamin V. was born in 1812 in Kaskaskia and came to Edwardsville with his family at the age of four. Edwardsville was really his hometown! Benjamin V. had the adventuresome Stephenson/Swearingen spirit. He ended up living in California, and I bet there wasn't a Stephenson mouse that had the nerve to travel that far!

Benjamin V. was living with his mother in Edwardsville when he volunteered for the Black Hawk War. He served as third sergeant in Captain Erastus Wheeler's Company of the Mountain Volunteers Brigade under the command of Major Samuel Whiteside. The enlistment of the men was for sixty days service and was mustered out at the mouth of the Fox River, Illinois, May 28, 1832. The group was 195 miles from Edwardsville, the place of enrollment. Now, did you really think Ol' Henry remembered all that? Nope, Elizabeth found all that information!

After the war, grandpappy Amos said Benjamin V. headed for Macoupin County where he was a surveyor. In those days many men who were raised on lots of land learned to be surveyors. In 1834 and 1835, he surveyed the town of Woodburn and laid out the town of Scottville. Benjamin F. Edwards, son of Ninian, was working with Benjamin V. at that time. Benjamin V. was elected Macoupin County surveyor in 1837 and 1839.

Now this guy moved around a lot. In 1839, he also lived in the Galena area; in 1840, he lived in Carlinville with his mother Lucy; and by 1842, he lived in Grant County, Territory of Wisconsin. Benjamin V. had purchased land in Carlinville from his mother, and the deeds show he lived in Wisconsin when he bought the land.

My Edwardsville cousin, Jake, says he remembers grandpappy Amos saying that from 1847 to 1849 Benjamin V. was a surveyor in Galena and lived in Howard's Boarding House. It appears he was not married at that time.

Henry remembers for sure that Benjamin V. took off for Yuba County, California, and in 1852, he applied for bounty land in California due him as a veteran of the Black Hawk War, and in 1854, he received eighty acres of bounty land in Yuba County, California. Grandpappy Amos said Benjamin V. sold the land to a Patrick Lynch in 1854 and then applied for additional land under a new bounty land act of March 1855. In 1856, Major Palemon Winchester wrote to the U.S. Pensions Office in Washington regarding Benjamin V.'s application for additional land. And, that my friends, was the last record that has been found about Benjamin V. Stephenson! I bet Karen and Amanda wish a Stephenson mouse would appear with the answers to the life of Benjamin V. Stephenson in California!

I have told you all Henry here knows about the Stephenson children at this time. But, the way my mouse relatives keep turning up with news, I just have a feeling that we will hear more about these children!

I sure will be glad when E. J., Keith, and Greg come back and start working on the tuckpointing. I really miss having them around! Right now I am going up to South Main Street to check things out. You know, Col. Ben owned some of that land long ago.

See ya' later,
Henry

A CASE OF MORTAR AND MALARIA

August 16, 2002

Looks like it is getting back to the way I like it at "my" house—there are people around again! Yep, Keith, Jack, and Greg are here, and they are tuckpointing the house. They started on the south side of the 1845 addition and are now working on the 1820 house. Looks great! The money from the Township and Mike Campbell made it possible to get the tuckpointing completed. A big thanks to the Township for investing in the Benjamin Stephenson House, the community, and Edwardsville's future generations.

The other day I heard Joe say that the paint tests show the house had not been painted before 1845. Folks, that means Col. Ben's house will remain unpainted, just like it was in 1820 and 1845!!! Also, be sure and take a drive through the alley and take a good look at the window that has been installed. It is called a 12 over 8 window, which means 12 panes on the top portion and 8 panes on the bottom portion. These are windows from another era, and you just do not see many windows of this style today. Do come by and see this absolutely gorgeous window! This style of window will be installed in the 1820 section of the house. The windows are made with one hundred-year-old glass, and this gives the slightly distorted look that existed in all early glass.

Henry here has heard Joe talk about the 1820 and the 1845 parts of the house from time to time, and the other day I heard him explain all about them. Col. Ben built his house in 1820 with two rooms down, two rooms up, and an attached kitchen. In 1845, the Wolf family removed the large original attached kitchen and replaced it with a two-story addition built on the foundation of the original kitchen. Now, here is what Henry finally understands: Col. Ben's 1820 house will be restored to the 1820 period, and the 1845 addition will be restored back to the 1845 period. Remember, the original woodwork, doors, and fireplace mantels have been saved and will be used in the house. Sounds awesome to me!

So, after the tuckpointing is completed in early fall, the windows will be installed and the shutters hung. I heard Carol describing the shutters, and they are just like the ones great-great-great grandfather Samuel talked about. The shutters on the lower level are a solid wood shutter because they were at ground level, and when closed they kept the insects and maybe an occasional raccoon out of the house. The shutters on the second floor are louvered shutters, which will allow the air to flow through. The downstairs shutters kept the vermin out, and the upstairs shutters allowed the fresh air to flow through. The way Henry sees it, today you folks have air conditioning, but in 1820 they had shutters that allowed the breezes to blow through the rooms. The windows were strategically placed to let the breezes come through.

Now, back to Col. Ben and the often-asked question: "What was the cause of Col. Ben's death?" Well, the other day Sid and Karen came by and they were talking a mile a minute. They had made a "find" in their research that leads them to believe that Col. Ben died of malaria. I really perked up my ears on this and listened carefully, and here is how I understand they came to that conclusion.

Sid had been studying the Stephenson records and saw where yellow bark, lima bark, and sulphur had been purchased just days before Ben's death. Sid found that yellow and lima bark are from the Cinchona tree and are the source of quinine. The bark was ground into a fine powder and mixed with water or wine and was the treatment for the fever of malaria. He also found out that long ago sulphur was used as a vapor to fumigate disease-infected rooms or homes. In the days just before Col. Ben's death, when the Stephenson's were buying barks used for the treatment of malaria, they also purchased four bottles of wine. We now know wine was used to mix with the ground bark for the treatment of malaria.

Dr. John Todd's bill for medicine and attendance was also found, and there is a big difference in the amount billed over several years. Karen said the total of the bill for two years, 1819 and 1820, was $28.25. In the year of 1821, the total bill was $44.25, and the bill for the ten months before Col. Ben's death in 1822 was $44.75. These figures also led Sid and Karen to think someone, probably Col. Ben, was having increased health problems.

Ol' Henry agrees with Sid and Karen's opinion that Col. Ben had malaria, which was either the cause of death or in combination with other ailments that may have weakened him. Good for Sid and Karen, now we have some clue as to how Col. Ben died!

Col. Ben died with his family at his side, and his son-in-law Palemon Winchester was the official witness of death. Dr. John Todd apparently was not present. Perhaps Col. Ben's death was anticipated, and the good Dr. John Todd could do no more for Col. Ben. The next day James Watts did the brick and walling of Col. Ben's grave and Samuel Thurston ridged the top of the coffin. Col. Ben's gravesite was fenced with palings, later called a picket fence, which were put in place by Watts. Col. Benjamin Stephenson had a burial befitting one of his stature in the community and in the State of Illinois. Probate records show a cost of $3.00 for bricking and walling the gravesite, $10.00 for the coffin, and $25.00 for the palings, which was very expensive in 1820. Great-great grandfather Ezra told us about his trip to Col. Ben's grave. Col. Ben was buried on Randle Street at the first public burial ground in Edwardsville. Col. Ben was laid to rest at the north end of this new cemetery at a quiet, peaceful place in the shade of trees and near a brook. Years later this cemetery was named Lusk Cemetery.

"My" house is looking so great with all that new tuckpointing — I am going outside to sit in the shade and admire the house. Keith mentioned the other day that the color of the mortar will get darker with time. You know, sometimes I think Keith knows I am here 'cause it seems like he makes sure I get extra crumbs. Life sure is good around here!

See ya' later,
Henry

GENERATIONS OF HOMEOWNERS

August 29, 2002

The hot, hot weather this week made me think of the old ice plant on South Kansas. Bet some of you remember that place. As a young mouse I sure enjoyed being there on hot days! Now, that was a cool place to be in hot weather! Hey, have you been watching "my" house? It looks to me like the tuckpointing is about finished and then the replacement windows will be installed and painted. Folks, this means the exterior work on the house is pretty well complete.

I heard Joe say the Friends are looking forward to moving into Phase II, which is the restoration of the interior of Col. Ben's house. With the help of you folks, Edwardsville, the State of Illinois, the Friends, and HPC are doing a restoration of the house. That word "restoration" means a whole, whole lot. Col. Ben's house is old and on the National Register of Historic Places, and the Illinois Historic Preservation Agency requires very specific materials and methods of workmanship in the restoration of a house as special as Col. Ben's. The Friends are in the process of searching for additional resources needed for the interior restoration through grants, in-kind donations, donations, and various fundraisers. The interior work includes electrical, heating, air conditioning, plumbing, and repairing the floors, the staircase, and some woodwork. Even the new plaster will be done very much like the original, which will include three layers of special types of materials.

Henry can easily see that this restoration work is a challenge for everyone. Henry can also see that the

Friends and HPC are excited about the interior work and are determined to make this place much like it was in the 1820s so that people will come from far and wide to experience life in the 1820s. Do the Friends ever rest?

The other day as I sprawled out in the grass trying to keep cool, I thought about the folks who have lived in Col. Ben's house. Of course, we know Col. Ben was the first, and now it appears that we know the date he and his family moved in! Sid found in the Stephenson probate records a bill for $5.00 from Jacques Mette for moving household furniture on December 15, 1821! Lucy and the younger children stayed there for more than ten years after Ben's death in 1822, but five of those years, Lucy's son-in-law William Starr owned the 182 acres of property. Her son James was the next owner who bought the property from Starr; then in 1834, James sold the Stephenson Homestead to Elvira L. Edwards, widow of Gov. Ninian Edwards. There isn't a mouse out there that can tell me if Elvira Edwards ever lived in the house when she owned it.

Ol' Henry recollects Uncle Thomas telling about Judge H. K. Eaton renting from Elvira when he came to town in 1836. Uncle Thomas said he remembered a baby girl, Amanda Eaton, being born in the house in 1836. He also said Judge Eaton retired to farming in Hamel, and Uncle thought there were a lot of Eaton descendants around the area.

Elvira Edwards owned the 182 acres for three years, and in 1837, she sold it to Thomas and Elizabeth Birks. The Birks owned the house for two years and in 1839 sold it to Philip Fix. He was referred to as "the valiant Napoleonic warrior" and led an interesting life. In 1845, Fix deeded the 160 acres, plus an additional 170 acres he had purchased to his only daughter Caroline for $1.00. One reservation in the deed was that he would occupy the second floor of the house until his death. He died twenty-three years later.

The day Fix deeded the property to his daughter, she deeded it to her husband Frederick A. Wolf. It sure did not take Henry very long to understand why Mr. Wolf built the addition to the house so quick. Caroline and Frederick had five children, her father occupied the second floor, which means they needed a lot more room for their family.

In 1880, Frederick A. Wolf, now a widower, sold the property along with additional adjacent land to his sons Adolphus and Frederick W. Wolf. Ten years later, Adolphus sold his share of the property to his brother Frederick.

J. Frank Dickmann bought the Wolf property in 1902, and the house remained in the Dickmann family for thirty-nine years, which was the longest any family had owned the house. In 1941, Elmer and Hallie Waltrip purchased the property. By this time most of the land had been sold off, and the Waltrips purchased just the home at 409 S. Buchanan. They lived there for two years, and then the Berry sisters, Stella and Ione, purchased the home, which provided the space needed for them to raise the orphaned children of their sister. The Berry sisters loved the house very much and lived there for almost twenty years. In 1975, the home was sold to Rev. Stephen Weissman and his wife Jacqueline. The Weissmans were a family who, like so many previous owners, loved and cared for the house. Rev. Weissman did the research that led to the Stephenson House being placed on the National Register of Historic Places in 1980.

Some of you may recall when the Weissmans sold the Stephenson House to the Sigma Phi Epsilon fraternity of SIUE in 1982. The fraternity owned the house until 1999 when the city purchased the home with

Illinois State grant funds. Since then, Henry has seen progress, progress, and more progress in the restoration of Col. Ben's house.

Someday Ol' Henry will tell you mouse stories about the various folks who lived in Col. Ben's house. I want you to "know" these folks like I do!

See ya,
Henry

COLONEL BEN'S CHARACTER

December 12, 2002

Yesterday, I was sitting back eating an apple I had saved for these cold days, and I got to thinking about Col. Ben and what I know about him. Who really was this man who is buried at Lusk Cemetery? What did he look like, how did his friends judge him as a man, and what role did he play as a politician and as a husband and father? Over the 180 years since Col. Ben died, stories of his life have gradually become forgotten memories. But, let Henry tell you that with Sid and Karen on the search for information on Col. Ben's political and family life, they won't quit 'til they find the information that is available. This all takes time, though, and slowly but surely a picture of Col. Ben will emerge.

Mr. Brink, the author of a respected history of Madison County, described Ben as quiet, unpretentious, and agreeable in his manners. He was a man who attended to his duties as receiver of the land office very faithfully. Brink wrote this in 1882 when there were folks around who had personal and reliable memories of Col. Ben.

Sid has recently located lots of information about how Col. Ben was elected to Congress, and now Henry understands how it all happened. Shadrach Bond resigned from Congress when he was appointed to the land office in Kaskaskia. Col. Ben was appointed to fill out his term as delegate from the Illinois Territory in 1813. On November 14, 1813, Col. Ben took Bond's seat in the U.S. House of Representatives. Well, Old

Samuel told us long ago that Col. Ben was elected to his second term. But, he didn't tell any details of the election and what went on. Maybe as a mouse he didn't find elections interesting! Remember what Henry has always said: Keep looking and the answer will turn up. And it has. Hey, the election story has been found! The secretary of the Illinois Territory was Nathanial Pope, and his records give us the story of the election. An election was held at the courthouse in Kaskaskia on September 1–3, 1814, for the election of a delegate to represent the Illinois Territory in Congress for two years. Here are the election results: "Benjamin Stephenson had one hundred and eighteen votes, and Joshua Oglesby had two votes for Delegate . . ." Looks like a landslide to Henry!

In June 1816, Col. Ben returned to Kaskaskia from his last session as a delegate to Congress. The last session of Congress had lasted from December 1815 through April 1816, and after a long trip home, he was finally returning to his family and to his social friends in Kaskaskia. Daniel Cook, editor of the *Western Intelligencer* in Kaskaskia, wrote about Col. Ben's role in Congress. Henry does not usually quote but you folks must read what Editor Cook wrote about Col. Ben:

> He has promised to use his best exertions to serve his constituents, but he made no display of what he was going to do — But what he has done shows his devotion of the people he represents. He made no parade of extravagant promises, but he has shown emphatically "his faith by his works" — We will not say that his success has been unexampled, but we may safely say that it has been very great, indeed unexpected — It shows that his vigilance never slept and that he must have obtained a character at Washington that

enabled him to serve his constituents. We may indeed say that he deserves well of his country.

Henry thinks these were mighty fine words of praise for Col. Ben. He must have been a quiet man who surprised his colleagues with his political abilities. Editor Daniel Cook's view of Col. Ben is one as his friends saw him as a man and a politician. It make's Henry happy to hear good things about Col. Ben.

In the same month of the newspaper article, Col. Ben wrote to a friend in Kaskaskia to tell of the good news that he had succeeded in getting all bills passed relating to Illinois. And, as expected, he gave credit to friends who helped with the success. Among those bills passed was a bill making the Wabash River a line of division between Illinois and Indiana; a bill to appoint a surveyor of the public lands of Illinois and Missouri; a bill to open a road from Shawneetown to Kaskaskia, for which $8,000 were appropriated; and a bill to establish a land office at the Madison County Court House (now Edwardsville). The letter concludes with a short paragraph by Col. Ben, and Henry is going to quote again.

> The foregoing bills passed in the same shape in which they were reported by the committees. I flatter myself that the result of my labors will convince my constituents that I have been zealously engaged in the promotion of their interests.
>
> (Signed) "B. Stephenson"

Well it sure appears to this mouse that Col. Ben accomplished a lot in his two terms as a delegate to Congress. The bills mentioned above are just some of the bills that Col. Ben succeeded passing in the U.S.

Congress. And, remember Illinois was still a territory.

Henry has more to tell you about Col. Ben, his days in Congress, and the bills he got passed. But, right now I am heading outside to search for more seeds and nuts to stash away for the winter. I just have a feeling that E. J. and his guys will be here soon. I gotta' get my work done so I can hang out with them when they get back.

See ya' later,
Henry

COLONEL BEN'S OBITUARY

March 5, 2003

Hey, hasn't the snow been fun? My cousin Jake and his grandchildren met me at the Public Library yard last time it snowed. Jake lives near the Klingel House, and this was a halfway point for us to meet. We all had fun playing in the snow! We even saw Sid going into the library to look up more stuff on Col. Ben. Henry thinks Sid is having fun doing this.

One item that Sid dug up was Col. Ben's obituary in the *Edwardsville Spectator*. Ol' Henry had a chance to peek at it and wants you folks to read the entire obituary. Hooper Warren, the editor of the paper, wrote the obituary expressing considerable sympathy for not only the family but also for all those who knew Col. Ben.

Edwardsville Spectator, October 12, 1822
DIED—In this town, on Thursday last, Col. BENJAMIN STEPHENSON, Receiver of Public Moneys for the Edwardsville Land District, in the 54th year of his age.

However unavailing the tear of regret, which is shed for a deceased friend—notwithstanding the efforts of philosophy, or the just, but ineffectual dictates of sober reason—it will flow. Vain to the bereaved widow and fatherless child are all the admonitions of careful friends—who fear and mourn rather for the living than the dead.

But when one who has filled the various stations of life with such pre-eminent faithfulness, as the subject of this notice, is called hence, the grief extends far beyond the precincts of the weeping relatives. All seem anxious to mingle their sorrows with the known pangs of the bereaved widow and children. Such emotions cause the present feeble attempt to sketch some of the events which have marked the life of Col. Benjamin Stephenson.

He was born on the 8th of July, 1769, in the then colony of Pennsylvania—whence he commenced his public life, and acquired the lasting esteem and approbation of all who knew him. In 1809, he removed with his family to Illinois, since which time he has filled various public offices, with such distinguished credit— so much to the satisfaction of all with, or for, whom he acted, that his eulogy is written in the hearts of more persons, perhaps, than will read this article.

During the late war he commanded a battalion under the then Governor Edwards, and a regiment under Brigadier General Howard, and in one or the other of which stations he was actively employed during nearly the whole period of danger to our exposed frontiers, and on all occasions distinguished himself so much by his vigilance, energy and intrepidity, as to secure the approbation of those under whom he acted, as well as the respect and esteem of those whom he commanded.

After the termination of his military duties, he was elected by the people of the territory to represent them in Congress. Without having become famous as a public speaker, he is acknowledged to have effected, by his prudent watchfulness, and through the esteem entertained for him, by his fellow members, as much at least as any other delegate could have done. From the high and honorable station Col. S. retired in 1816, having received the appointment of Receiver of Public Moneys in this land district. In this station he continued to retain the confidence, friendship, and esteem, it is believed, of all who knew him. As a member of the convention which formed the constitution of this state, his conduct was especially satisfactory to his constituents.

Although the writer of these lines has known and honored the deceased as a public officer, he has to state that it was in the friendly and domestic circles that the virtues of his heart shone with peculiar lustre. If the patriot mourn his death as a public loss—if friends shed the tear of sorrow over his grave—what, oh! what are the agonies of a beloved and affectionate wife—now wife, alas! No more, and of children, cherished by the kindliest sympathies of paternal love?

He alone who is the widow's God, and Father to the fatherless, can heal the wound which His hand, in his own wise providence, has made. To Him may they look in humble confidence, and in Him may they find present and eternal consolation.

This was certainly an obituary written by one who was deeply saddened by a death. Warren wrote a moving article about the highpoints of Col. Ben's life and a touching rendering of the deep grief of his wife and children. Immediately upon his death the words of praise, respect, and friendship for Col. Benjamin

Stephenson were spoken with great compassion. Warren's choice of words such as confidence, faithfulness, respect, esteem, and friendship describe a man we would all have enjoyed knowing. Great-great-great grandfather Samuel said that October 10, 1822, was a very, very sad day.

Among other things that Old Samuel mentioned was that Warren and Col. Ben had some opposing political views, which in those days could develop into pretty heated arguments. However, Hooper Warren obviously liked and respected Col. Ben so much that in death he could easily put the political issues aside. Henry thinks these were two exceptional men.

The weather has been snowy, it has been bitter cold, and it has rained, and you know what? E. J. and the guys can't do much on the house in that kind of weather! Henry here is getting a lot of time to sleep and think, but I sure will be glad when activity starts around here again. Guess I will go take a nap, again!

See ya' later,
Henry

THE COLONEL IN CONGRESS AND A TALE OF AN INDIAN ABDUCTION

March 19, 2003

Ol' Henry here and Cousin Jake have been putting our heads together to remember the stories great-great-great grandfather Samuel told about when Col. Ben was delegate to Congress. We've remembered a lot!

It was Old Samuel who spun many a tale around the time when Col. Ben decided not to run for re-election to Congress. Great-great-great grandfather Samuel told about Col. Ben writing a long letter to the folks in the Illinois Territory about his two terms in Congress. This letter was published in the Kaskaskia newspaper in June 1816. The letter told of the laws Congress had passed for the benefit of the Illinois Territory, and Old Samuel would chuckle. He knew it was Col. Ben who saw and heard what the Illinois Territory needed and had introduced the laws and succeeded in getting them passed. Old Samuel chuckled because Col. Ben was pretty closed mouth about what he had accomplished, but most people understood.

Col. Ben's first day in Congress was on Nov. 14, 1813, and only eleven days later he introduced two resolutions. Not bad for the new boy in Congress! One resolution was to employ more militia in our area for the War of 1812, but the war soon ended, so it was withdrawn.

The second resolution involved matters about land and land grants. The law on the land matters had nine sections, so it covered a lot. Old Samuel said Col. Ben made sure the settlers who had settled in the Illinois Territory before the land was surveyed and for sale would be treated fairly. Col. Ben proposed that if these early settlers who had settled on free land could show they had occupied and improved the land, it would be legally their land, and it could not be sold by the federal government. This resolution was passed into law by Congress.

This resolution about land also included wording about land claims made by men who had served in the militia. They were entitled to land grants if they had a warrant certifying their service. These land warrants could also be purchased. Thomas Kirkpatrick, one of our first settlers, purchased his land warrant from Pierre Lejoy, a Revolutionary War veteran.

Col. Ben also proposed in this land act that folks could be granted land because of sufferings from treatment by the Indians. Col. Ben told in his letter published in the Kaskaskia newspaper that he had secured land for Mrs. Ann Gillham as compensation for her suffering while a prisoner of the Kickapoo Indians. He said he could have done the same for others if he had been provided with the proof needed. Henry here has heard that the story of Ann Gillham is told in Brink's History of Madison County. But, the story great-great-great grandfather Samuel told long, long ago is the one that Henry knows.

One day in 1790, James Gillham and his small son Isaac were plowing his cornfield in Kentucky. While Gillham was in the field, a band of Kickapoo Indians sneaked into his house and took his wife Ann and their other three children as prisoners. The Indians ripped open the feather beds and used the ticking for sacks to carry the stuff they stole from the house.

The Indians hurried off with their prisoners, avoiding white settlements along the way, hurrying forward without food or rest toward the Kickapoo town near the headwaters of the Sangamon River in Illinois. Old Samuel said he heard Mrs. Gillham tell that after they crossed the Ohio River on three rafts of dry logs, they started moving slower and found food. Finally, after traveling a long way, they reached the Kickapoo Indian town at Salt Creek, about twenty miles from today's Springfield, Illinois.

Old Samuel said it was a terrible scene when James Gillham returned from the field to his house. He saw the feathers from the beds scattered all over and his wife and children gone. The frontiersman knew his family had been taken by Indians. Gillham and his friends immediately started to trail the Indians and they found footprints of Mrs. Gillham and her children in several places, but soon the trail was lost. Gillham sold his property in Kentucky, and went to Vincennes and Kaskaskia hoping the French traders who had knowledge of the Indian tribes could be able to help him. However, at this time the whites and Indians were very hostile, and little information was to be found. After five long years Gillham heard from a French trader that his family was with the Kickapoo Indians. With guides and two French interpreters, Gillham visited the Indian town at Salt Creek. He found his wife and children alive and well! A ransom was paid through an Irish trader named Atchinson at Cahokia. Great-great-great grandfather Samuel said the youngest child could speak no English, and it took some time before he could be persuaded to leave the Indian country.

In 1797, two years after finding his family, Gillham became a resident of the Illinois Territory. The action of Congress in 1815 gave Ann Gillham her choice of any available quarter section of land within the Illinois Territory in testimony of the hardship and suffering she had endured during her captivity among the Indians. Ann and James Gillham settled on 160 acres of land near Long Lake in Madison County in 1815.

Well, Col. Ben did a fine job getting the land laws

passed quickly by Congress. There are other areas where Col. Ben provided a lot of help for the folks in the Illinois Territory that I will tell you about later. He really achieved a lot in his two terms in Congress.

Here is some good news we all have been waiting for! Mark and his men are here at "my" house and have started work on the electrical part of the heating and cooling system. E. J. and his crew will be here any day, and let me tell you, when they get here my food situation will definitely improve. I like the summer sausage from the Market Basket and so do they!!

See ya' later,
Henry

INGREDIENTS TO A SUCCESSFUL RESTORATION

April 16, 2003

As I keep saying, things are really moving along at a fast pace at "my" house. From what I overhear from Carol and Joe, Mark the electrician has the electrical and ductwork on the inside of the house completed. Good job, Mark and crew!! Now my buddies, E. J. and his crew, are back. I am so happy to see them and their good food! They are digging the foundations for the porch and smokehouse. The smokehouse should be a pretty neat hiding place, not only for the heating and cooling equipment, but for me too!

OK folks, time for a little restoration talk. All of you realize that the work going on at the Stephenson House is a true restoration, right? Believe me, it is a once-in-a-lifetime opportunity to witness such a restoration. Why once in a lifetime? Let Henry here tell you the reasons. Number one, there aren't many 1820 brick houses around to restore; number two, it takes an incredible amount of money; number three, it takes a group of truly dedicated, knowledgeable, and energetic volunteers to get this sort of project going and completed; and, number four, the group needs good guidance.

Well, folks, we have it all! Edwardsville has one of maybe five 1820 brick homes in Illinois. In 1998, Edwardsville was most fortunate to receive a grant of $500,000 from the state through the efforts of former Senator Evelyn Bowles. And, to put this all together, Edwardsville has a group of dedicated and knowledgeable people at the Edwardsville Historic

Preservation Commission and the Friends of the Col. Benjamin Stephenson House. These folks are giving their time and dedication to this project, and they love it! Some have been working since May 1998, the very month it all began. Good guidance on the restoration has been provided by the Illinois Historic Preservation Agency and architects Jack and Laura.

Edwardsville had the house, it received the grant, and now it has the people who are willing and able to oversee the project. And, the Edwardsville community is providing the support needed. What a wonderful place to call home!

All those working on the Stephenson House are grateful for your support. But, they want you to see this restoration, follow it, and understand the work that is being done. One day in the near future, these volunteers will present the completed 1820s restoration that will be a true jewel for the City of Edwardsville and the State of Illinois.

Right now, Henry here says we must also keep looking at what Col. Ben accomplished as a U.S. congressman. When we look closely at Col. Ben and his goals, we get a glimpse of his persuasive abilities. We also get another look at Ben as a person.

One of Col. Ben's major legislative accomplishments was getting the War of 1812 militia paid. Our Col. Ben worked until he was satisfied that the secretary of war and the paymaster for the army would pay the men without delay. It was the federal government's responsibility to pay the militia, and this was a big, big problem because there was almost no federal money. The War of 1812 had seriously hurt international trade, and import duties were over three-fourths of the United States income. So, the government was hurting bad!

The pay issue was solved when a resolution presented by Col. Ben was passed. This resolution allowed the militia veterans to receive a pay certificate from the army paymaster that could then be used in any government land office to pay for land. The idea came from Illinois Territorial Legislature, and our Ben got it passed in Washington.

Ben had been able to convince the secretary of war and the army paymaster to pay the militia with a land certificate! Col. Ben's persuasive powers appear to have been considerable to get that agreement.

Here is a story Cousin Jake recalled hearing. The Illinois Militia was being paid with land certificates, and the Missouri Militia had not been paid. Hey guys, this payment issue was the hot item of the day! Illinois was being paid, and Missouri was not. The *Missouri Gazette* carried a letter in 1816 signed "A Ranger" who asked why the Missouri Rangers had not been paid. Could it have been because the Missouri delegate had less influence than any other delegate or member to congress? "A Ranger" was clearly dumping the failure of pay for the Missouri Militia on Rufus Easton, the territorial representative from Missouri.

Henry and Cousin Jake were talking about this pay thing the other day. The militia had been promised they would be paid to protect the people, but they had only received delay, expenses, and refusal. The militia included the Illinois Rangers, and two of these four companies were commanded by local men, Samuel Whiteside and William B. Whiteside. The rangers furnished their own equipment and horses when they ranged between settlements, spotting danger. They kept the Indians off balance, hit hostiles before they struck, pursued those who had attacked, and provided protection for the isolated settler. The rangers were to be paid one dollar per day, which was good pay, and Col. Ben, with the rank of major, was to receive one dollar and sixty-seven cents a day. The militia was understandably upset! But, Col. Ben solved the matter in Washington. He did a lot of good things for the average guy.

See ya' later,
Henry

SOME SWAP HELP

April 30, 2003

You know what? The activity still goes on at "my" house! As you drive by you see all that is going on outside. Hey, there is also the inside!

Early the other day the Madison County Sheriff's Work Alternative Program—I call them the SWAP boys—arrived at the door. "My" house was on Norm's list of places that had asked for help, and his people were here and ready to work early in the day. Henry here could see Joe working with Norm's people, and they got a lot done. The Friends sure do appreciate all the help from SWAP!

What a day it was! After the guys removed some ugly stuff on a couple of the upstairs ceilings they made quite a find! In the 1820 childrens' bedroom, the original pine rafters were uncovered with some of the original bark on them. And, Henry really liked this next thing. Have you ever heard Joe talk about the sheathing boards under the roof? Now, with the ugly stuff off the ceilings, we can really see those sheathing boards. The boards are ten to twelve feet long and eighteen inches wide. Those are some big boards, huh?

Each sheathing board is a solid, one-piece board cut from a very large and very tall tree. Can you imagine the size of that tree? Our skilled craftsman friend, Joe H., who knows about lumber and the old days, thinks the tree was a sycamore. Sycamores grew to be huge and were readily available to be cut down and lumbered or planked near the site of the house. I heard Joe H. say that the carpenters probably built a 6' × 8' frame, put the tree trunk on it, and two men used a two-man ripsaw to "lumber" or plank this huge one-piece sheathing board. Madison County did not have any steam mills to help with these big jobs until 1832. You all must take a look at these sheathing boards the next time "my" house is open for a Take-A-Peek! They are impressive.

Norm, Sheriff Hertz, and the SWAP people sure make Ol' Henry wake up and take notice. It seems that each time you guys give us a hand around here something really old and interesting is found. Lieutenants Terry and Bob are lucky because they are always one of the first to see the discovery! Hey, I was here the day that one of the SWAP workers brought his son to "my" house to show him this old, old house and to tell him about all the history that happened here. Henry liked to see that! Henry watches you all from my hiding places, and it makes me happy to see and hear you enjoy "my" house.

Henry has been telling you about Col. Ben's accomplishments as a delegate in Washington. Now I am going to tell you about one bill he got passed that I think will be interesting to you. Col. Ben sponsored the bill that, when passed, authorized the president to lease the salines for an additional seven years. What were the salines? Well, salt came from saline springs. Salt was enormously important at that time because salt was the only way to preserve meat. The object of the bill, when enacted into law, was to assure that the most salt possible was being produced, not only to meet the demands but also to help reduce the price. Once again, Col. Ben was there accomplishing what the folks needed.

In the early days, salt beef and salt pork were sold by the barrel. Now, that requires a lot of salt—and just where did it all come from? The major source was the salines just west of Shawneetown. Clay pans that the Indians had used for evaporating the salt brine had been discovered, and this helped government surveyors locate the two potent salt springs near the Saline River and Shawneetown. Sid said this is near today's town of Equality, Illinois.

Now, how does one make salt from the saline spring water? Salt production was hard work. Water from the salt springs was led to cast iron kettles through hollowed logs used as pipes. Long lines of kettles filled with the salt water were boiled over log fires. Henry heard Sid say that one authority said 125 to 280 gallons of boiling water were needed to produce one fifty-pound bushel of salt. And, 80 to 100 bushels of salt were produced in one day at the salines! Now, how many gallons of boiling water does that take in a day??

Because the need for salt was so great and producing it so labor intensive, the salines were exempt from the prohibition on slavery in Illinois. An authority on the salines said there were from 1,000 to 2,000 slaves who worked in salt production at the salines. Most of these slaves were leased from their Kentucky and Tennessee owners. The slaves cut and hauled the firewood, scooped the salt into barrels, and loaded it onto carts. Oxen hauled the bushel barrels of salt to Shawneetown where it was reloaded into keelboats headed to markets in Indiana, Tennessee, Kentucky, and Missouri. Men from Illinois rode over one hundred miles for a packsaddle load of salt. Remember, salt was the only means of preserving meat. Salt was enormously important!

The salines produced at least 120,000 bushels of salt each year, and it cost between eighty cents and one dollar per bushel to the buyer. The salt production from the salines was so important that Congress set up a ten- by thirteen-mile reservation for the protection of the timber that provided the firewood. The salines near Shawneetown were leased by the federal government, and Territorial Governor Ninian Edwards served as superintendent of the U.S. Salines, the official name of the salines. The income from the salt supported a great deal of the Illinois territorial government. Salt was important for many reasons!

This exception to the antislavery rules at the salines gave the proslavery people hope that the prohibition would be overturned, and at the same time the antislavery folks kept a real close eye on the management of the salines. Even after the territory became a state, and Illinois prohibited slavery, the salines continued to be an exception until 1825. Hey, isn't Henry so smart to know all this? Actually, Sid and Karen found it in a book, and I heard them talking about it!

See ya' later,
Henry

A CAPITAL IN FLAMES

May 14, 2003

Henry here has been thinking too much about Col. Ben and the bills he succeeded in having passed in Congress. I needed a break! So, I took a stroll over to see the new road on South Main. You know, that land was part of Col. Ben's original 182 acres, and great-great-great grandfather Samuel spent a lot of time in those fields. All of a sudden some stories Old Samuel told about Col. Ben as a delegate in Washington came back to me.

Old Samuel was at Kaskaskia when Col. Ben left there for Congress in October 1814. Since Illinois was not yet a state, Col. Ben was delegate, a non-voting participant who represented the Illinois Territory in the U.S. House of Representatives. To get the important bills passed for the Illinois settlers, Col. Ben needed many friends who had a vote in the House. Col. Ben knew he had to convince his friends of the importance and necessity of the bills he introduced. Old Samuel knew Col. Ben was the right man for this job, and he was right!

Hey guys, the War of 1812 did not end in the year 1812! On August 24, 1814, the British burned Washington, D.C.! They burned the public buildings, the Capitol, and the White House, home of President James Madison and his wife, Dolly. The city was a smoking ruin.

Old Samuel had heard Col. Ben tell about the British burning Washington and the rebuilding of the city. He told about Col. Ben arriving in Washington and seeing what some called a "naked city." He told about the buildings being built far apart and the few streets being little more than paths. The farmers were even fencing in fields and planting in places meant to be streets. Everywhere Col. Ben looked the public buildings had been burned. The treasury, navy, and state departments, the Library of Congress, and the executive offices were burnt out. By the time Col. Ben arrived, the government had found temporary quarters in private buildings around town for most of these departments. Some private Washington homes were loaned for use as executive offices.

Old Samuel recalled that Col. Ben was happy to tell that the Patent Office had been spared the torch because the British finally agreed with the Americans that its contents belonged to all civilizations. The Post Office was spared because it was in the same building as the Patent Office.

On September 19, 1814, less than three weeks after the burning of the capital, President Madison called a special session of Congress. At this session, Congress voted to restore the burned out Capitol and to pay for the repairs. It was decided that Congress would be temporarily housed in the Post Office Building. At the same time, a group of thirty-eight citizens offered to build a brick hall as a temporary Capitol. Within six months, the building was erected, and Congress met for the next four years in the "Old Brick Capitol." When Col. Ben arrived, there were some citizens who felt the city was in a defenseless position, and they urged the moving of the capital to Philadelphia, Lancaster, or Georgetown. Col. Ben felt that the group of private citizens who were building the temporary Capitol showed a united spirit that helped keep the government in Washington.

When Col. Ben accepted the appointment as delegate in 1813, he knew he was taking on a big responsibility to the people of the Illinois Territory. And, this also involved personal hardships for Col. Ben. His travel time was thirty-five days to Washington. The congressional sessions lasted 140 days. He was away from his family in Kaskaskia for almost six months at a time. For all this, Col. Ben was paid eight dollars per day plus mileage. Many considered Washington an unattractive city, with buildings and houses so far apart it was called "the city of magnificent distances." Old Samuel said he heard that people had to travel four, five, and six miles to a home to attend a dinner party.

So what did Col. Ben think when he arrived at a city in ashes? Old Samuel said it really didn't matter to Col. Ben, because he had come to serve the Illinois people and would continue to serve under any conditions.

Old Samuel said there were 176 congressmen in town for each session. Where did they live? Over the years the Stephenson House mouse family had learned about the hotels, boardinghouses, and taverns where the congressmen stayed while in Washington. The average charge per night was sixteen dollars for a hotel room. Many of the congressmen stayed in boardinghouses called "messes" that were rented only by congressmen. These boardinghouses mostly clustered around taverns, probably because the taverns were the social center and the place for many gatherings. In 1822, there were thirty-one boardinghouses and certainly fewer in 1813 when Col. Ben was in Washington. Great-great-great grandfather Samuel said he thought about forty congressmen stayed in boardinghouses during Col. Ben's time. Old Samuel could not recall where Col. Ben stayed. He was getting older, you know! However, he figured Col. Ben was one of the congressmen who stayed in a boardinghouse.

After Col. Ben's arrival in Washington, a story came back to Kaskaskia about a visitor to Washington who said the appearance of our public buildings was enough to make one cut his throat! Washington must have been a pitiful sight! When the British burned Washington, they also unwittingly succeeded in uniting the Americans to defend their country, and national pride was revived! Historians Samuel Morison and Henry Commanger said: "The destruction of Washington only showed that invading a country like the United States is like hurling a hammer into a bin of corn. A few kernels were hurt, but the hammer had to be withdrawn quickly or lost."

Col. Ben was proud to be part of the rebuilding of Washington while serving his fellow people in the Illinois Territory. Colonel Benjamin Stephenson was a true public servant, and Illinois was fortunate to have him. You know, Henry thinks he was really good!

Gotta' run,
Henry

FROM WASHINGTON TO EDWARDSVILLE

May 28, 2003

"My" house is buzzing with activity again, and I bet you don't realize how much is going on. I do for sure! Why? Because I see all the different men coming and going in their trucks and coming into "my" house with all their tools. I see all this from a place where I can hide and watch as they work. But, every time I settle down in what I think is a safe spot, someone appears near me to measure for a pipe, mark a place for a drain or a shut off valve, or run a wire for a motion detector. I just have to move on to another spot! This all says that the security system is being installed and plumbing is about to be a reality. Progress is at work, and Henry is busy staying out of the way.

Well, now it's time to go back to the story of Col. Ben's days as delegate to Congress. There are just a few bills left that I want to tell you about. One is the bill Col. Ben introduced that resulted in the regulation and definition of the duties of judges in the Illinois Territory. This new bill provided for a circuit court system that required the judges to hold court twice a year in each of the counties. The legislature of the Illinois Territory was authorized to determine the time and place of court. This was really important for the settlers. Previously, the court met only in Kaskaskia, and it was extremely expensive and difficult for many folks in the territory to reach the courts. The three judges in Kaskaskia were not pleased with the new bill, however, because it required them to travel, and they felt they were not paid enough to travel.

One of the bills provided for a new road from Shawneetown to Kaskaskia. Now, I heard all the old timers talk about the roads. Great-great-great grandpappy Samuel told how the roads were poor: muddy in the rainy season, dangerous when raging rivers caused flooding, and dangerous when night came.

The overland trail that George Rogers Clark almost lost his way on in 1778 was still used to reach Kaskaskia from the south in 1816. This was an overland trail that had been cut by the hooves of buffalo. Can you imagine what kind of "road" that must have been! It was Col. Ben who got a bill passed to open a road from Shawneetown to Kaskaskia. The bill, funded for $8,000.00 called for cutting the road thirty-three feet wide, with very low stumps. This was the first federally funded road in Illinois!

Another bill that Col. Ben sponsored was an act to establish a land district in Illinois Territory, north of the district of Kaskaskia. This bill was passed April 29, 1816.

Henry here would like to remind you about Col. Ben's letter in June 1816 to the citizens of the Illinois Territory explaining what he had accomplished in Washington. He felt the people deserved an explanation of his activities in Congress. Col. Ben wrote a rather humble, informative letter that told us about Col. Ben's successes as a delegate to Congress. He told the citizens about the bills Ol' Henry has been telling you about.

Col. Ben said he felt he could do more in Congress in the future. He spoke of how he was now familiar with the proceedings in Congress and of his large circle of friends and acquaintances in Washington, who helped him succeed in getting bills enacted. Col. Ben called it a "melancholy truth" that a delegate of a territory could not be very successful in getting bills passed without friends and acquaintances. Remember, a delegate of any territory did not have a vote in the U.S. House of Representatives; therefore, he needed cooperative friends.

Ol' Henry wants you all to slow down and give some thought to what politics were about in 1816. The Illinois historian John Moses was quoted in 1914 as having said that the position of a delegate to Congress in 1813–1816 was not highly desirable. Moses said it was desirable only as a steppingstone to something higher.

The men of the Illinois Territory knew the land was being surveyed and would soon be for sale. This would require another Land Office to handle the number of sales. Col. Ben, who was obviously a well-known and respected figure in Congress, was ready to make a change in his life.

The letter Col. Ben wrote to the Illinois Territory citizens was dated June 19, 1816, and it was his final act in his congressional career. He was not returning to Congress, even though he knew he could exert more influence than during his first two terms. When he wrote his letter, President Madison had already appointed him receiver of public money at the Edwardsville Land Office. And, on May 11, 1816, Josiah Meigs, commissioner of the General Land Offices, had confirmed Benjamin Stephenson's position.

It was Col. Ben, the delegate, who worked for the welfare of the Illinois Territory and who introduced the bill for the new Land Office. The Land Office was very important to the growth of Edwardsville and brought many men of importance to town. Just to give you guys an idea how important the receiver of public money was: Henry has heard that the governor's salary was $1,000 a year, and the land grant receiver of public money received around $3,000 a year, depending on the revenue from the sale of land.

The appointment allowed him to return to his family in Kaskaskia and move to Edwardsville, which became a center of political activity in Illinois. The Land Office sure did bring a lot of men to Edwardsville who were instrumental in developing the State of Illinois. Many of them lived here at one time or another and included men such as Daniel Cook, Edward Coles, Ninian Edwards, James Mason, Jesse Thomas, Joseph Conway, and Abraham Prickett. Col. Ben was on the horizon of an active political career in which he continued as a true public servant.

Various letters between the U.S. Treasury Office and Col. Ben reflect that his salary was hard earned. And, Col. Ben and Lucy built what certainly was their dream home in Edwardsville.

See ya' later,
Henry

WOMEN'S RIGHTS IN THE 1820s

June 27, 2003

I know I keep talking about "my" house to the point that you all must think I am bragging! I am just so happy with "my" house, and I want everybody to hear about it and also come by and see the progress. There sure is lots to be proud of around here! The porch has a great ceiling, a new concrete floor, and I hear the columns should be arriving soon. The smokehouse is looking good, and I am anxious to see it when the spire is on the roof for the final authentic touch. We sure are lucky we had the probate records that showed that Daniel Tolman had made a spire for the smokehouse!

Hey, here is a question, and Henry here wonders if you know the answer! In what year were women allowed to own property in the State of Illinois? This question has been asked often, and Stacey at the Papers of Abraham Lincoln in Springfield gave us the answer. Stacey told us that women in Illinois could always own property. It was when a woman married that she gave up her right to own, manage, or sell property. Oh, oh!! When a woman married she became legally invisible and took on her husband's legal personality. In short, all property was now in the name of the husband. Hmmmmmm, says a girl mouse, what a bummer!

Karen asked why Lucy was named and signed deeds of sale if she did not own the property. The answer is that the wife signed because of her right of dower. If and when the husband died, the widow was the manager of the property. The property buyer was aware of this and wanted the wife's signature on the deed so that there would not be a problem with ownership if she was widowed and was managing her share of the property. Just to be real sure the wife was not being forced into agreeing to the sale of property, the court official questioned her in private, to be certain the sale of property was okay with her. You see, there was the possibility that the husband would sell all the property without the wife's knowledge, and she would be left a pauper if he died or disappeared. Golly, the wife and the buyer both had to be very alert!!

The married woman was legally invisible, but as a widow she suddenly found ground to stand on. Now, Henry will do his best to explain what he knows about the widow's right of dower. I am just a mouse, ya' know! Dower was the right of the widow to hold and manage one-third of her deceased husband's estate during her lifetime, and this gave her some financial security. So, the widow was the manager of her deceased husband's property. The widow did not own the property but held it for life. At her death, her one-third dower went back to the estate and the heirs.

A widow could buy and sell additional property in her own name. This did not affect her dower right.

So, ladies, here is the bottom line: If a woman remained single she could buy and sell property. When she married she could no longer buy and sell; she could only use her right of dower to influence her husband's decisions about property. As a widow she could manage her one-third of the estate—her dower right—and receive the profits, but she could not sell this property. A widow could buy and sell additional property in her name just like she did when she was single. Gosh, maybe she could use the profits of her dower and buy more property in her name!

As a widow, Lucy Stephenson received her one-third dower right. The researchers are searching, but right now no one knows the extent of her dower right after Col. Ben's death and the probate settlement. Ol' Henry does know that Lucy was one sharp lady, and when she moved to Carlinville she bought property in that area. Some of that property she later sold to some of her relatives. Lucy was a widow for twenty-eight years, and Henry here thinks that she invested wisely in property.

Well, we now have another question answered about life in the 1820s in Illinois. Henry says thank you to Stacey!

OK, did you all have a good time at the "Taste of Downtown Edwardsville"? I sure had a good time and stayed way late, searching for tidbits of good food from the restaurants. Mary and her committee did an outstanding job and deserve many, many cheers!!! Henry loved seeing so many people visiting with friends and enjoying the food and music as they supported the Stephenson House. Everyone, and I mean everyone, was raving about the decorated Transit Center and how beautiful it looked! The red, white, and blue flag decorations were absolutely great, and when the lights came on at dusk, the Transit Center was transformed into a wonderland. Talk about ambiance!

July 13 and Ben's Birthday Party are coming up soon. Yes sir, there will be homemade ice cream and cake for Col. Ben's birthday. Mary and her committee will be ready for the occasion. Henry here has heard that many of Col. Ben's relatives and friends will be dressed in authentic clothing from the 1820s. Now this is a party you do not want to miss!! Ol' Henry can't wait to see how the folks dressed back then. Sure hope you stop by, and if you care to bring a gift for Col. Ben he could use a little cash in any amount because he needs a new staircase in his house. Maybe we can all help him out in his time of need! Oh, by the way, the Stephenson House will be open, so come Take-A-Peek!

I am heading for the smokehouse for a nap!

See ya' later,
Henry

COLONEL BEN'S BIRTHDAY

May 23, 2003

Let me tell you, Ben's Birthday Party was great! There were lots of people here enjoying ice cream and cake as they wished Col. Ben a happy birthday. Mary, her committee, and a lot of the FBSH Board members had "my" house in tip-top shape. They had the windows sparkling clean, and yes, you are right, it was George who mopped the floors. The living room was a step back to the 1820s with the antique furniture and antique accessories on the mantel and tables. The breeze wafting through the open windows completed a beautiful picture of Col. Ben and Lucy entertaining in the 1820s.

Henry saw lots of you folks at the party, including Bob, Henry, and Shirley; Esther, David, and Mary Deane; Corrine, Betty Jean, and Jean. I watched as you all were enjoying the ice cream and that super delicious cake of Dottie's. And, I listened as you talked with the folks dressed in 1820s clothing! I counted seventeen of Col. Ben's visiting friends and relatives in their beautiful, authentic clothing, and they were enjoying the day!

You can see that the FBSH Board loves to give parties! This one was rather special in that contributions could be made to a fund for Col. Ben's new staircase. Well, once again you all were very generous and contributed over $1,600. The people of Edwardsville have a wonderful sense of history and a tremendous community spirit. Col. Ben loves it and so does Henry!

The researchers received another nice surprise. It was a letter written by Col. Ben to Daniel P. Cook on

April 22, 1815. It was written as Ben was on his way back to Kaskaskia from his first session in Congress. Ben wrote from Summerset: "I arrived here this evening with my family, the road is extremely bad, in four days more I expect to reach Pittsburgh, when I intend to take water to Ferguson's ferry." In the letter, Col. Ben asked Cook to rent him a home at Kaskaskia: "Get any house that you think will answer, we won't be particular for the present." He also told Cook that he needed a place for a hatter's shop. A young man was with Ben, and he wanted him to "go to business immediately." Ben also had the equipment with him that would be needed for the hatter's shop.

So, it appears that Lucy and family did make the trip to Washington with Col. Ben in the fall of 1814. The researchers have never been too sure if she went with Col. Ben or not. Then just the other day good old Cousin Jake came up with some recollections! Jake recollects that great-great-great grandfather Samuel used to tell how excited Lucy got when she found out she could visit her relatives and enjoy seeing her children meeting their aunts, uncles, and cousins. The Swearingen and Stephenson relatives lived in Martinsburg and Shepherdstown, Virginia, and both towns were almost right on the way to Washington. It seems just logical that she did not go to Washington but took this opportunity to visit her family.

It is doubtful that Lucy would have stayed in Washington with Col. Ben in 1814. The stories Ol' Henry heard about the streets, the living conditions, and the social life in Washington—plus the condition of the roads just to get to Washington at that time—were scary! Most members of Congress did not bring their wives and families until around 1850. Sure sounds to Henry that Col. Ben brought his family home to Kaskaskia after they visited relatives in Virginia.

Congress had recessed for almost a month before they headed back to Kaskaskia. It appears the Stephensons spent some time in Virginia before they began their trip home to Illinois.

Ol' Henry had an idea the researchers would get real busy after Col. Ben's letter was located and figure out where the places were that Col. Ben had mentioned. I was right! Summerset is in Pennsylvania and is on the way to Pittsburgh from Washington and Virginia. Now, that was easy. The location of Ferguson's Ferry took a little more time, but after some searching on this new thing called the internet and studying old maps the researchers had the answer! Ferguson's Ferry was in today's town of Golconda, Illinois. It was a trading post and the first major place to come ashore after leaving Pittsburgh on the Ohio River! After a brief rest there the Stephensons had to return to water and the Mississippi River to reach Kaskaskia. In 1815, there were no roads inland from Golconda, so travel by water was the only way to reach Kaskaskia. Good for our researchers, they found the answers!

Right now I am waiting for the columns for the porch to arrive—they will be awesome! Folks, Henry is sincerely glad you took time for another look at Col. Ben's house. I keep telling you, do not miss this restoration as it progresses!! When the upstairs area is ready for a group, you must visit the rooms and see how the beams and wood were used for the roof. You know, in the near future all this wonderful old brick and the interior roofing will be hidden from view forever with plaster.

This has been a big weekend, and I am going to go enjoy a long, long nap.

See ya' later,
Henry

A FALSE ACCUSATION

August 8, 2003

This old mouse is so doggone proud of "my" house and all the folks who have worked so hard with the restoration. Just take a look at the smokehouse! There are wrought iron strap hinges on the doors that were hand forged by Bob Woodard. The design is a bean design that was very popular in early America. They are magnificent! And, the smokehouse has been sided with an old-fashioned siding called slip-siding. This siding is of pine that was kiln dried especially for the smokehouse. The smokehouse with its hand-forged hinges and slip-siding is one example of why "my" house is so authentic. Keith and his crew found an 1820s piece of pine here at "my" house that had been protected from the weather. Well, Joe found a wood stain that matches the old pine. The smokehouse is now the natural gray color of untreated old pine, and it will weather beautifully. It is people like Joe and Keith with their ideas, inspiration, and dedication, that have made Col. Ben's House, "my" house, a beautiful, warm home!

Gosh, I was surprised the other day when a big group of men and women came to "my house." I overheard Carol, Elizabeth, and Donna talking, and Henry here understands that our Mayor Gary is president of a mayors group and that the visitors were Illinois mayors and their wives. They had come to see Col. Ben's house! Henry wants everyone to see Col. Ben's house, and I sure am glad they were here! The girls had refreshments for the visitors at a beautiful table set with flowers from the 1820s, and Sid gave the folks a great tour, as he told them all about the house and its history. After the mayors left, Ol' Henry just sat back and smiled. They loved "my" house. The house is looking so wonderful!!!

More good news has arrived for the researchers. A researcher from Chicago found a copy of a letter from Wm. H. Crawford replying to a letter he had received from Lucy Stephenson! Who was Wm. H. Crawford? He was secretary of the U.S. Treasury! He was the big boss of Josiah Meigs, commissioner of the Land Office, and Col. Ben, receiver of moneys at Edwardsville. He was the man Lucy wrote asking why Palemon Winchester, her son-in-law, had not been appointed to take Col. Ben's place as receiver of moneys at the Edwardsville Land Office. As receiver, Col. Ben had reported to Josiah Meigs, his immediate superior, and Meigs reported to Wm. H. Crawford. Since both Meigs and Col. Ben were deceased, Meigs shortly before Col. Ben, Crawford was now the only person left who had knowledge of Col. Ben's office.

As the first receiver of moneys at Edwardsville, Col. Ben had a very big job. On behalf of the government he sold new frontier land in the Illinois Territory. The land was sold at very reasonable prices because the government was in dire need of funds for its operation. This new large expanse of land was governed by new, untried reports and regulations, and men had to work under entirely new circumstances. Plus, the distance between Washington and Edwardsville was far and communications were very, very slow. Mistakes were made by all, and political enemies were made as well.

Secretary Crawford's June 14, 1823, letter responded to each of Lucy's questions, which is how the researchers discovered Lucy's questions. Ol' Henry heard Sid and Karen discussing the letter, and this old mouse had to concentrate real hard to remember what they said. Crawford said President James Monroe had decided against Winchester as the new receiver of moneys. He said the president had made his decision based on the information that he (Crawford) was including in his letter. It sure looks like he wanted Lucy to believe he was not involved.

The first information provided by Crawford was that Lucy and Winchester had declined to administer Col. Ben's estate. Now, Ol' Henry talked with Cousin Jake, my cousin who seems to know everything! Jake said his side of the mouse family often talked about Lucy's letter, and he knew some of the old stories. He said the fact that Lucy and Winchester declined to administer Col. Ben's estate led to false rumors! Folks in Edwardsville knew Col. Ben was suffering before his death and was unable to get the land sale accounts for September and October written and sent to Crawford before his death. Well, Jake says some of the folks in Edwardsville still got all upset when Lucy and Winchester, her son-in-law, declined to administer the estate because some knew Lucy had those two months of land office money in her possession. So, the rumors really began to fly! The story that Lucy and Winchester were defrauding the government of the land sales money spread quickly. Eventually, Crawford had heard the rumors and passed them on to President Monroe.

Lucy said in her letter that she still had the land sales money as "proof" that these rumors were untrue. Lucy did not know what to do with the land sales money, but she did know that Crawford had forbidden Col. Ben to put any money in the Bank of Edwardsville for various reasons. With the passing of Meigs, Lucy had no one to direct her. She asked Crawford for the reason no one had contacted her to give instructions for the money. Crawford's answer was that she should get the money to the new receiver of moneys, and he would provide a voucher that would clear Col. Ben's account with the government. That was a good answer, but it failed to acknowledge that Lucy did not know the identity of the receiver until April 1823, about the time she wrote her letter to Crawford. Communications were very slow in the 1820s!

Edward Coles had resigned as registrar of the Land Office in 1820, and the records do not show a registrar appointed to the Land Office until January 1823. It appears Col. Ben was the only government employee at the Land Grant Office, and Lucy was waiting to hear from Crawford or someone in Washington about the handling of the receiver's accounts. Lucy and Winchester, who was an attorney in addition to being her son-in-law, waited for instructions from Crawford while the rumors flew that they were defrauding the government.

Crawford also supplied President Monroe with the information that Col. Ben had "misapplied" a portion of the receivers money a few months before his death. Cousin Jake remembers many of the old stories about this "misapplied" money. He explained that Col. Ben was expected to pay the Kickapoo, the surveyors, Captain Boltinghouse's militia company, and other legitimate government expenses. But funds were not always allocated for these payments. So, some payments were made without waiting for permission from the government. Crawford apparently expected the Kickapoo to patiently wait for payment while authorization letters were going back and forth between Col. Ben and Crawford. These letters could take two months each way! Cousin Jake said the Stephenson mouse family even laughed at that.

The last bit of information Crawford gave to President Monroe was that Col. Ben had not sent in the accounts for land sales from September and October 1822. Crawford had to know that Col. Ben was sick during September and died October 10, 1822, but still reported to the president that there were irregularities at the Edwardsville Land Office.

Well folks, what do you think about Lucy, a young widow in 1822, questioning Wm. H. Crawford, secretary of the U.S. Treasury, about presidential appointments? Henry here thinks she was quite a woman, especially for the 1820s. Lucy was educated, intelligent, and obviously a woman who stood up for what she thought was right. Lucy, her husband, and her son-in-law had been unjustly criticized by the U.S. Treasury, and she took her position against the secretary and demanded an answer. However, her questioning letter did not change the appointment. Samuel C. Lockwood, apparently the man Crawford wanted, was appointed receiver of moneys of the Land Office in Edwardsville in February 1823.

The many Edwardsville receivers letters that Sid has located have helped to understand some of what Crawford wrote to Lucy. One thing that is known for sure is that the many receivers letters from Meigs and Crawford never even hint that Col. Ben did anything dishonest.

Hey, a little girl dropped a bag of corn chips in the alley a few minutes ago! I am going to spend my evening with corn chips!!

See ya' later,
Henry

MISS LUCY'S LATER YEARS

September 4, 2003

I'm just hanging out at "my" house trying to keep cool. Most of my excitement has been when Jim and Sid were here making a sign for the 50/50 Auction coming up this Sunday. It should be a good auction—don't miss it!

I was having an easy, laid back week, and the next thing I know Cousin Seth appears, coming all the way from Carlinville! He had heard how great the restoration was coming along, so he came to see for himself. He was impressed! Well, you know how it is, we got to talking about Col. Ben and Lucy once again. I learned a lot as Cousin Seth recalled the stories great grandpappy Amos told about Lucy's death and what was reported in her obituary. Ya' know, it was great grandpappy Amos who hid in the bureau drawer so he could move to Carlinville with Lucy in 1834. He stayed with her until her death in 1850.

Cousin Seth began his stories with Lucy's death. She was sixty-one years old when she died at the home of her grandson-in-law, Nicholas Boice, who was married to Miriam Winchester, daughter of Palemon and Julia. Great grandpappy Amos said Miss Lucy died after suffering a long and complicated illness. He said the family did all they could do, but the pain and suffering could not be controlled or conquered.

Cousin Seth said Old Amos got tears in his eyes when he told how alert Miss Lucy was as she neared death. She remained calm as she gave final advice to her children and selected her funeral hymn. Then Miss Lucy died quietly. Grandpappy Amos loved Miss Lucy, and he knew she was an exceptional woman until the end of her days.

Ol' Henry asked Cousin Seth about Lucy's obituary, and he said it told that Lucy was born in a fort near Wheeling, Virginia, married Col. Ben, came to Kaskaskia, and finally to Edwardsville. The obituary told that Lucy, a widow for twenty-eight years, was a friendly, good-natured woman. She was kind and thoughtful and was known to think before she spoke or acted because she was not only thoughtful but also very cautious. Miss Lucy was highly valued as a friend, parent, and grandparent.

Elvira, Lucy's widowed daughter, was in Carlinville to care for Lucy when she was sick. Cousin Seth recalls that there were a lot of folks at Lucy's house to help care for her. Elvira was there with Lucy's granddaughter, Laura Winchester, who along with two other girls, ages seven and twelve, were there to help care for Miss Lucy, according to Seth. Miss Lucy was ill for a long time. And, her living children—Julia, Elvira, and Benjamin V.—were near her during her illness and with her when she died in 1850. Lucy was moved to the home of Nicholas and Miriam Boice just before she died. Lucy Swearingen Stephenson died on August 28, 1850, in Carlinville. Cousin Seth learned from Sheila that Miss Lucy's obituary, written by Dr. J. A. Halderman, was published in the *Alton Telegraph and Democratic Review*.

Right now I am really looking forward to the 50/50 Auction this coming Sunday, September 7. It is going to be so much fun, and I hope the Friends make a lot of money to help with the restoration of "my" house. Seems to me that they are on the verge of being able to open and have activities for kids and grownups. I hear Carol and Joe talking, and I know that they " just" need to get that plastering done and some other things taken care of, like woodwork, locks, and ceilings, and to get the courtyard paved with brick so you folks do not have to wade in mud after it rains! And, the best part is that when the house is open to the public, the Friends will be eligible for grant money from various places that will enable them to present excellent programs.

See ya' later,
Henry

UNEXPECTED DISCOVERIES!

October 1, 2003

So many things have happened at "my" house that my head is spinning! We now have water lines and spigots installed on the lot, and Jim, Sid, Rose Marie, and Carol planted grass seed that Jason provided. Thanks, Jason! I saw Jim watering the seed the other day, and it is turning green! I have heard that painter Bill will be here soon to paint the windows and all the trim on the house and the columns and ceiling on the porch. I was promised that it will be fun having Bill around here! The other day Joe took the guys in a truck to pick up the millwork that had been stripped in St. Louis. Soon I will really have company when the board members are here getting it sanded, primed, and painted.

My buddies E. J. and his crew are back! They are busy getting the concrete base ready for the brick courtyard and the foundation for the summer kitchen poured. And, the guys brought the finished house shutters with them.

Let me tell you about the biggest discoveries that were made last week. Contractor Christ Brothers from Lebanon had started to work on the parking area. They began digging trenches for the curbing, and of course, when you say "dig," Sid, the archaeologist, immediately appears, and it sure was a good thing he showed up. The foundation of Col. Ben's barn was found!! That is the truth as sure as my name is Henry! Sure enough, Sid identified a brick foundation sixty feet from north to south and at least forty feet from east to west. The remainder looks like it's under the alley. They found great big limestone rocks at the corners of the barn that were used for added support for the building. Sid and Joe are pretty sure the barn was made of wood and that it burned down because they found charred remains as the digging progressed. Can you imagine the excitement! Carol, Joe, and Sid were celebrating over the discovery and taking pictures. Me, I was just running around in circles, trying to remember if I had heard any stories about the barn. What a day that was!

Everybody wished they could keep the foundation uncovered so a lot of folks could see it, but work has to go on. Although the new find was covered and the curbing poured, Sid came up with some ideas on how maybe a part of it can be kept visible.

The foundation of the barn confirmed that the Stephensons led an elegant lifestyle because a barn with a brick foundation was an extreme luxury in the 1820s. Remember, back then a lot of people lived in log cabins with dirt floors! The Stephenson animals had a wood barn with a brick foundation just like the bricks made right here for Col. Ben's house! Jim came over when he heard about the barn, took one look, and said it was right in the barn area where he found a horseshoe the day they were clearing and seeding grass! I get so excited talking about it that I just get the shivers!!

Ol' Henry is wondering when the barn burned or came down. I'm sure the researchers are going to find some answers! Isn't this exciting!

Why stop with the barn though! In all the excitement, there has been another discovery by the alley!

The Stephenson privy was found!! Man o' man, what a find! Digging was going on for the handicap parking lot, and the next thing you know they were finding brick walls that were in a large rectangular shape. Well, they found a 9' × 6' privy, and everyone is sure that it was built by the Stephensons because it is made of the same brick as the house and the barn foundation. Now, let me tell you, that is a big privy! Ol' Henry's heart was beating loud and strong! This mouse has heard about privies, and I know this is where you find all kinds of things that belonged to the family because the privy was also a place to throw broken and unwanted objects. Wow!

Sid was there when the privy was found and plans were made to excavate the site. I heard somebody say that pieces, called shards, of china from the 1790s have already been found! Henry here thinks Sid is really having fun!

Henry here has not heard the complete details of the Burgoo. However, I do know that there are going to be some young men here digging two fire pits for the Burgoo. Yes sir, two pots of Burgoo this year, and I betcha' it will be all gone by the end of the day. Wilma Jene and Lois will start cooking very early in the morning, and the Burgoo will be ready at 1 p.m. on Saturday. Sounds good to me—of course, I like that great bread and freshly churned butter too. Hope to see you there!

See ya' later,
Henry

MOVIN' IN

December 23, 2003

'Tis the night before Christmas and all through the house, not a creature is stirring—not even Henry, this old mouse. I found a cute little red hat that I know Mary left here just for me, and I'm wearing it now. It's just me, Santa Mouse, curled up in my hidey place watching the glow the beautiful new post lantern creates on the front yard. Life is great!

Way back in 1820, the folks did not celebrate Christmas, because that celebration came years later. December was just another month—usually a cold one. However, in December 1821, there was one family in Edwardsville that was very busy and happy. The Col. Benjamin Stephenson family was very busy, because on December 15 they were moving into their new brick home!

I heard Karen say there is a bill from Jacque Mette in the Probate Records that tells the story. In early November 1821, Mette delivered seven loads of wood and one load of beef to Col. Ben. During the first weeks of December, Mette's bill shows that he "hauled . . . 1 load of barrels—$2.00; 1 load of plank—$.25; 2 loads of barrels—$.50; 1 load barrel and meat—$2.00; 2 loads of hogs—$.75." It looks like the Stephensons were making sure they would have plenty of food, livestock, and firewood in place before they moved in. On December 15, Mette finished his part of the move when he hauled the household furniture, total charge—$5.00.

On December 15, 1821, the Col. Benjamin Stephenson family spent their first night in their new home. How happy they must have been! Henry wonders if it was snowing on the new home and all the outbuildings. Just imagine the beautiful scene in rural Edwardsville.

Mette returned the first of January with five more loads of wood. The wood probably came from Col. Ben's property, and Mette charged twenty-five cents a load for hauling. Wonder who cut the wood?

Jacque Mette, the hauler, is a story himself. In 1812, Mette was one of the persons Governor Edwards had arrested in Peoria for "assisting the savages to murder our frontier settlers." He was among the prisoners brought to Fort Russell. Apparently, Mette became "rehabilitated" by 1819, because at that time he was living in Edwardsville and served as official interpreter for the Treaty of Edwardsville, working with Auguste Chouteau and Col. Ben. Mette must have been really "rehabilitated" for Col. Ben to have trusted him to haul all of the Stephensons' worldly goods to the new home in 1821.

You all know about warm fuzzies? Picture the Stephenson family gathered around the fire, enjoying their first night in their new brick home. That is a warm fuzzy!

HAVE A MERRY CHRISTMAS
AND
A HAPPY NEW YEAR!!!

See ya' in year 2004,
Henry

RETAIL AND MERCHANDISE IN 1820

January 8, 2004

Hi! Henry the Stephenson House mouse is back again and glad to be back with you in year 2004! Henry here had surprise visitors who came knocking at my door the other day. They were my Cousins Seth from Carlinville, Jake from here in town, and Elzey from Columbia, Missouri. They came by to check out the progress of the restoration of "my" house.

So, Ol' Henry gave them a tour, pointing out the beautiful brickwork on the new porch that now has columns, the parking lot, smokehouse and the new windows and doors. They were happy to see the new furnace do its job and keep us all nice and warm. Gosh, there was just so much to show them! The barn foundation and the privy, recently discovered, were a highlight of my tour! I sure wish Sid had been around so he could have told them firsthand about privies and what he found in the one at "my" house. They loved the tour and the first comment they all made was "impressive."

Each cousin has lots of Stephenson family stories to tell. Cousin Jake recalled a lot of the stories great-great grandfather Ezra told about the ads in *The Spectator*. The first issue of that paper was in early May 1819. We expected to see ads about Col. Ben's store, but we didn't realize that he was closing his store at that time and was not advertising. The big advertiser was Robert Pogue who had "A splendid assortment of MERCHANDISE." Pogue's store, located where Rusty's is today, had everything! Cousin Jake said

Pogue advertised that he had for sale prime green coffee, sugar, pepper, allspice, raisins, cinnamon, nutmegs, cloves, and Irish Glue. Hey, do you know what Irish Glue is? The cousins think it was glue used by the Irish dancers to keep their socks from falling down! Wonder if they're right? Now, if you were looking for liquor, Pogue offered port wine, Madeira wine, cognac brandy, N. E. rum, Holland gin, and whisky. Henry thinks that Pogue had a big store.

Robert Pogue had supplies such as nails, bar iron, pig lead, plough irons, and axes. He also had pots and pans, tin kettles, Dutch ovens, and skillets. There were scythes, bottles, saddle bags, bridles, and horse whips for sale at Pogue's store. And, the person who wanted school books could find them at Pogue's, along with writing supplies. He had ink stands, common paper, letter paper, ink powder, and quills.

When the ladies needed fabric, Cousin Jake said Pogue had a big selection. Superfine black, blue, or brown cloth, superfine and common "cassimeres" (the way cashmere was spelled), Russian linen, and Irish linen were offered for sale and advertised in *The Spectator*. Pogue had bed cords and bed ticking, coarse and fine domestic shirting, fancy and plain domestic cottons, and straw bonnets. And, Pogue even carried a general assortment of medicine!

As Cousin Jake said, the Pogue store had it all! Robert Pogue and his brother had two stores, one in Edwardsville and another in Carlyle. We cousins got to calculating, and we figured that Edwardsville was about fifteen years old and had only about sixty homes in town. Robert Pogue was probably carrying all that inventory not only for Edwardsville but also for the settlers and the Indians coming from far and wide to shop at the Pogue store. Looks like his store was the supermarket of the day!

We got to chuckling about how Pogue sure knew how to please his customers. He had superfine cloth, coarse and fine shirting, and fancy and plain cottons. He had fabric that was priced for many different needs and, importantly, pocketbooks. Men could buy fine and coarse shoes or Best Black Morocco leather shoes, and that same man could choose from the best fur hats, common hats, or leather hats. We mouse cousins thought no one complained because Pogue aimed to please all people's tastes and pocketbooks!

Cousin Seth popped up with a couple ads for lost items that were in the 1819 *Spectator*. One was an ad placed by a man who had lost a Red Morocco pocketbook that contained notes "of lend" on several people. The other ad Seth recalled was for a saddle with plated stirrups that was covered with buffalo skin and a cloak of new green plaid with an otter skin collar that had been lost between Edwardsville and St. Louis. Both advertisers offered liberal rewards for the return of the lost items. These ads in *The Spectator* for lost items and the Pogue store advertisements made Ol' Henry and Cousins Seth, Jake, and Elzey think Edwardsville had a real mix of people with a wide difference of money available to buy Pogue's merchandise.

Cousin Elzey had heard long ago about *The Spectator* advertising items from the Subscriber, a store owned by W. C. Wiggins and located opposite the Bank of Edwardsville. Listen to what Elzey said they had for sale! How about pickled salmon, pickled shad, codfish, tongue, and smoked herring? This food was pickled to keep it preserved for the long trip to Edwardsville. W. C. Wiggins must have gone to a lot of effort and expense to get these pickled fish for his customers.

Ol' Henry is just amazed with how much the cousins remember from all the old mouse stories! Cousin Jake mentioned that Abraham and Isaac

Prickett operated a store in Edwardsville in 1819 too. Jake can't understand why they didn't advertise in the paper. Jake said Abraham did run an ad that said: ". . . the customers will recollect that business cannot be done without money. Those that take the hint will call at the store of Isaac Prickett & Co. and settle their notes and accounts without delay."

My cousins have gone back to their homes, and I am here thinking about all the food advertised in 1819! I guess Ol' Henry will be heading out to see what I might be able to find for supper.

See ya' later,
Henry

PLASTERING THE HIDEY PLACES

October 7, 2004

Hey, hasn't this been some great weather? Cousin Jake dropped by with some of his grandkids the other day, and we all just hung out around here and had fun playing in the leaves. There sure is a lot to catch up on around here, but it is the plastering that got my attention real quick. It covered my hidey places. Can you believe that?

Henry here has been hanging close to Keith and Jack, and I have learned lots about plaster. Yeah, plaster! I heard them talking about the three coats of plaster that were used in Col. Ben's house in 1820. The first coat was a heavy plaster made of lime and sand that stuck to the brick walls. Then the second coat was put on. Can you guess what was in that plaster? Hair! Henry here is telling you it was all kinds of hair, including hog, horse, and even human hair. This hair was combined with sand and lime, which made the nice straight walls and ceilings. The final coat was a finer coat that was nice and even.

Let's talk about this hair in the plaster. Now, if you all think a little, you will remember that nothing was wasted in early America and especially not on the frontier! When Col. Ben and his friends trimmed the tails and manes of their horses and when they butchered hogs and other animals, they saved the bristles from them too. Also, people saved the hair they cut from their heads. Henry guesses that the guy who did the plastering may have even paid for the hair when he gathered it from the folks who saved it. There were more animals than buildings at the time, so there was plenty of hair for the plasterer's needs.

Today, it is a different story, and there is no horse or hog hair in the plaster. Today's plaster is made of sand, cement, and lime. Seems to Ol' Henry that those are some of the ingredients in concrete for sidewalks as well.

Henry has been keeping an eye on how Keith and Jack do this plastering. They have almost finished all the rooms in "my" house, which is a lot of plastering! They call the first layer a scratch coat, and it goes over wire mesh that is on the brick walls. This coat doesn't have to be as heavy as the first coat in the 1820s homes because it clings to the mesh, not the bricks. Then the guys scratch all over this coat with a tool, leaving grooves in the plaster. Next, they put on the second layer, which they call a brown coat. Henry has no idea why it's called brown. The brown coat contains some fiber instead of horse or hog hair! This second coat bonds in the scratches and fills in the voids or uneven areas. This coat is the one that provides the nice, straight walls that are then covered with the finish or hard coat, made of lime and cement — no sand — and this is the final coat we see.

Ol' Henry heard Keith telling Joe that the plaster has to dry or "cure" for thirty days before it can be painted or wallpapered. You would think this time would give everyone a chance to rest. Well folks, some of this plaster has already been finished for thirty days and has cured, which means it is ready to paint. So, Joe and Chuck will be there on Tuesdays giving the plaster a primer coat. Henry is proud to be around all these guys who work so hard on Col. Ben's house!

Now I'm hearing talk about painting the millwork and mantels and about what color paint will be used! Henry learned that in 1820 the color of paint used in houses was a whole lot different than what we use today! I am anxious to find out what colors will be used in Col. Ben's house. I heard Joe say something about a paint analysis that had been done on the original millwork in the house, which allowed us to tell what color Col. Ben and Lucy had painted everything in 1820. I do not know what an analysis is — I am just a mouse ya' know — but if Joe says it will tell us what color paint Col. Ben and Lucy used, I will believe him for sure!

Now, I am on my way to the garden. I wonder if Carol F., RoseMarie, and Jim thought of me when they chose the seeds they planted? I know the sunflower seeds are mighty good, and I will check to see if they are ready to eat! Just in case you are wondering, I am still sleeping in Keith's truck, and it is a nice place to sleep. Hidey places are hard to find around here!

See ya' later,
Henry

LUCY'S EARLY YEARS

October 22, 2004

Golly, do I love this time of year when the sun is warm and the fallen leaves are wonderful and crispy to run and play in. It's a perfect time to show off "my" house, so I asked Cousin Jake to drop by. So many new things have been done while we were on vacation, and I wanted to give him the grand tour. Well, he was impressed and especially liked the sunflower seeds in the garden as we toured the grounds.

Ol' Henry also told Cousin Jake that he will be extremely impressed when the staircase is installed! Yep, I hear that the staircase will soon be here. I overheard Joe and Chuck saying that the next work to be completed is the staircase and that Keith and Jack will be back when it is ready to be installed. A staircase in "my" house, now ain't that grand?

Hey, Ol' Henry is anxious to start telling you about our big vacation! Cousin Jake and I hitched a ride on a plant truck that was leaving the Market Basket and, low and behold, it went straight to Columbia, Missouri. Talk about luck! We found Cousin Elzey in no time flat, and the fun began as we explored, ran, played, ate scrumptious food, and met all the Stephenson mouse relatives in Columbia. There sure are a lot of them. Naturally, we reminisced about the old Stephenson days, and this is when I met Cousin Isaac.

Cousin Isaac is really an interesting mouse. He is a balding, skinny old fellow who barely can see and uses a cane to stay on his feet! But, he is one sharp dude who tells great stories. He had new stories to tell about when Lucy was growing up, which were told to him by his great-great-great grandpappy Josiah who lived at the fort in Wellsburg, Virginia, where Lucy was born in 1788.

Before Lucy was born, "Indian" Van Swearingen, Lucy's father, built his fort on the banks of the Ohio River in Virginia. Today, that area is the town of Wellsburg, West Virginia. Cousin Isaac's stories paint a real picture of life on the Ohio River when Lucy was young. The Revolutionary War ended just four years before Lucy was born. Her father had fought in that war, and he also fought the Indians in the frontier along the Ohio River. The white man was coming west to the Ohio River Valley, and for many years the river was the scene of bloody fighting between the white men and the Indians. Lucy grew up hearing talk of the Revolutionary War and lived through the years of fighting with the Indians. Her older half brother, Thomas, was killed by Indians when he was out hunting. This tragedy occurred shortly before Lucy was born, but the story was familiar, since it was told over and over as her father grieved. The last white man killed by Indians in Brooke County, the Wellsburg area, was in 1795. Lucy was seven years old.

Lucy's older sister, Drusilla, was married to Samuel Brady, the famous Indian scout in the Ohio River Valley. Brady would leave on scouting trips for long periods of time, and Drusilla and her two children would be left alone at their home near the fort. Lucy no doubt realized the fear Drusilla experienced for her husband, herself, and the children during their separation.

Lucy Swearingen Stephenson was one plucky lady, says Ol' Henry. She left all the turmoil she had grown up with and headed for the new frontier at Kaskaskia in the Illinois Territory. The War of 1812 on the horizon surely had to bring back memories of all the Indian fighting along the Ohio River and trigger fear in Lucy's heart. Yes sir, she was one plucky lady!!

Cousin Isaac also told us a new story about Lucy's father's will. "Indian" Van Swearingen died in 1793 and willed land to all his children, along with certain bequests to each child. To his son Van he bequeathed "one mulatto boy by the name of Isaac generally known by the name of Tobe which is to become free at the age of twenty eight years." Well, that is when Henry here jumped up to add to the story! I remember great-great-great grandpappy Samuel talking about Tobe after he arrived with Lucy from Kentucky. He said that Tobe was twenty-three years and nine months old when Col. Ben registered him as an indentured servant in 1809 at Kaskaskia. Old grandpappy Samuel said Tobe's term of indenture would be up in four years and three months, when he was twenty-eight years old. Well, by golly, when Col. Ben registered his people in Madison County in 1817, Tobe's name was not there. He had reached twenty-eight years of age and was a free man.

Cousin Isaac agreed with Ol' Henry that Tobe was probably the same Tobe that was willed to Lucy's brother Van. Cousin Isaac said that Lucy and her brothers Thomas and Van did some trading on the property left to them in their father's will. Thomas and Van were Lucy's natural brothers from her father's third marriage to Eleanor Virgin. The other brothers and sisters were from his first and second marriages. It sure was good to talk to Cousin Isaac. He is a character full of facts, fun, and advice. Well folks, I am on my way across the street to Dairy Queen's parking lot to see if anyone has dropped any food. I have eaten a lot of sunflower seeds and am ready for a change in diet. A hot dog on a bun sounds mighty great!

See ya' later,
Henry

THE ROILING POLITICS OF EARLY EDWARDSVILLE

April 7, 2005

Hey, once again there is lots of progress to report at "my" house. All the rooms have been painted, including the foyer, and the children's bedroom is completely wallpapered and looks beautiful! Keith and John, the painters, have been wallpapering the master bedroom, and Keith has glazed the woodwork. Those two have put a special finishing touch on Col. Ben's house! And, of course, the Paint Crew is great to watch. They do so much and move so fast that I am sure to keep out of their way!

Henry here is ready to tell you a story about Theophillus Smith and Hooper Warren and how some political disagreements were handled in early Edwardsville. But, let me fill you in with some background first.

You all might just recall that there was a big question about slavery for many a year in our country. There were those who wanted slavery in the new state of Illinois and others who did not. *The Spectator*, printed in Edwardsville by editor and owner Hooper Warren, was the most influential, widely read newspaper this side of the Allegheny Mountains from 1819 to 1826. It was a very loud voice against slavery coming from Edwardsville.

Now, there were men who owned indentured servants. These people had previously been known as slaves, but new laws were passed. Indentured servants had agreed to serve their owner for a certain number of years, and then they would be given their freedom. That is the way it was. The men in Edwardsville who owned indentured slaves included Joseph Conway, Benjamin Stephenson, Ninian Edwards, John McKee, John Todd, and Nathaniel Buckmaster.

Well, great-great grandpappy Ezra never, ever mentioned slaves or indentured servants in his stories. Ol' Henry and Cousin Jake learned about all this during my visit to Lower Town recently, and we did a lot of reminiscing. We remembered some of Ezra's stories about how happy Hark was when he would get a new store-bought shirt from Miss Lucy. And Ezra told about Dottie who would dance around in the new shoes that Miss Lucy bought from Isaac Prickett's store. Cousin Jake and Ol' Henry think we didn't remember or pay attention to those stories because we could not figure out who Hark and Dottie were. Henry here now remembers Joe and Sid talking about the probate records and the bills for clothing and medicine for Col. Ben's indentured servants. It seems they did mention the names Hark and Dottie.

Actually, Cousin Jake and his buddies in Lower Town really had a lot of discussions about the long-ago slavery question. There were two sides to the issue, and the Stephenson House mouse relatives know very little from great-great grandpappy Ezra. The few stories passed down show that Col. Ben and Lucy took very good care of their indentured servants. We were happy to hear that, and we decided to drop the talk. I am just a mouse ya' know.

Now to the Warren and Smith story. Hooper Warren owned *The Spectator,* an antislavery newspaper, and Theophillus Smith owned the *Illinois Republican,* a proslavery newspaper. As you can expect, this created heated political discussions, and altercations often occurred.

The story goes that one day Theophillus Smith appeared at Warren's office armed with a dirk—that is a dagger—and a whip. He was prepared to do harm to Warren. Smith saw that Warren was armed with a pistol, and he retreated from the office. Emmanuel J. West happened to be waiting, and he convinced Smith to return to Warren's office where West attempted to be peacemaker between the two newspapermen. Warren said Smith could come in the office if he would behave. Smith agreed to behave, and then the two men attempted to get each other to write an acknowledgement that the other had no personal knowledge of anything derogatory to his character. The problem was who would go first!

Before this attempt to make written peace with each other, Smith and Warren had made a mutual surrender of arms at the urging of Mr. West. Well, as Warren was writing, Smith got to Warren's pistol and emptied the powder out of the priming pin.

Hooper Warren then refused to make peace. Theophillus Smith—knowing Warren had no weapon, went after him with his whip and dirk. Emmanuel J. West prevented any injury to either man. Wow! Politics in 1824 Edwardsville!

A lively little story about Hooper Warren and Theophillus Smith! Henry here now understands why great-great grandpappy Ezra's stories about politics were few and far between.

The sun has been shining, and the tulips are coming up. The herbs are turning green and growing. I am headed outside to see what else has made its appearance in "my" yard. I heard Carol and Jim talking about planting some roses just like the ones that were around in the 1820s. It will be fun to see what they look like.

See ya' later,
Henry

THE GREAT 1811 EARTHQUAKE

April 20, 2005

Hey, the grape arbor is underway!! Jim and Carol F. planted six big grapevine plants in the backyard. The grapevines will climb up the arbor and bring back visions of long ago when the Wolf family made wine with the grapes they raised here. Do you think our grape arbor with six vines will bring winemaking back to "my" house?

It has been a busy week for Keith the painter and Keith the carpenter, one finishing the glazing and the other replacing the deteriorated floors in the 1820s part of the house. Everything sure is looking good! The electrician was here and hung some beautiful light fixtures in the hallways, bathrooms, and the back stairs in the 1845 part of "my" house. He also installed track lighting in the orientation room. This mouse understands that if you want light in the 1820s part of "my" house, then you will use candles just like Col. Ben and Lucy did long ago. Henry here just knows that candles will create beautiful light and bring a wonderful glow to all the rooms.

The Paint Crew was telling stories as they painted the 1845 floors, and I heard George talking about the Earthquake of 1811–1812! Ol' Henry scampered to his hidey place and listened to every word said. George had been reading about the earthquake, and Henry heard him say there were actually four big quakes in Southern Illinois. There were two on December 16, 1811, one at 2:15 a.m. and one at 8:15 a.m. The other two were in January and February 1812. George said there are numbers that rate how bad an area is hit by an earthquake. He saw a map that showed Kaskaskia and Carmi, Illinois, and Louisville, Kentucky, were given ratings of 6, 7, and 8. Only New Madrid—which is along the fault line—got an 11 on the December 16, 1811, earthquake. I am just a mouse, ya know, but it sure sounds like a rating of 6, 7, and 8 meant the area was hard hit.

George said that the earthquakes were felt for about four months. Reports of the trembling earth came all the way from the Atlantic Coast. Hey, that included New York City, New Hampshire, the Carolinas, New Orleans, and of course, Tennessee, Kentucky, and Illinois. There are many stories from all these areas, including one from a man in Louisville who recorded 1,874 separate quakes between December and March. He sure was a busy guy keeping those numbers! There were lots of stories, lots of changes in the land, rivers, and lakes but, as George pointed out, very few lives were lost.

According to George, the old stories told how the ground would shake and then rock and roll in long waves. After a quiet spell, there would be another shake and a long roll. During the long continued roll, the tops of the tall trees would tangle together. As they swayed, they would part and fly back the other way. Then the tangled top branches would pop like gunshots when they broke, and the forest floor was just covered with broken limbs. George said that when he says "tall" he means the kind of tall timber that made ninety-five-foot logs! Wow!

Why didn't the log cabins fall apart when the ground moved? Well, I asked Charles, a buddy of Cousin Jake, and he told me that these houses were like pens about fifteen feet square and seven feet high, built of small logs that one or two men could handle.

These logs were dovetailed at the corners, and long logs were used to support the roof. On one side was a door and on the other side there was a six-foot square area about a foot deep for the "chimbley." It was built out of many small layers of split white oak sticks and wet clay, with one half of the chimney in the cabin for the hearth and the other half outside for the base of the chimney. Charles went on to say that the houses "in the country" were built with wood and wet clay, with no nails and no stones. Actually, these houses were flexible like a basket and were a perfect structure to resist an earthquake.

Jake's buddy Charles had stories to tell about how the earth heaved up piles and piles of pure white sand on the plains that covered many square miles near the Wabash River. He said that all the stories agree about how frightened the domestic animals were. The horses were nickering, cattle lowing, hogs squealing, and mice squeaking, all running to the house for protection and comfort.

Kaskaskia was the area Ol' Henry was most interested in during the "great shakes" in 1811–1812 because Col. Ben and his family lived there. Well, guess what? Sid had an article about the folks in Kaskaskia! He read it out loud so everyone could hear:

> The folks at Kaskaskia were frightened beyond description by the earthquake as the earth waived like a river blown by the winds, the church steeple bent like a reed and the old bell rang like a demon was pulling the rope! The houses cracked like it was doomsday and stone and brick chimneys fell down. The earth cracked open with crevices so deep that folks could not hear a stone hit the bottom! The air and the water drawn from the split earth had a terrible, disagreeable odor. The people of

Kaskaskia, believers and unbelievers, flocked to the church and listened as the stout old priest implored mercy from Him whom the elements obey.

Now, at last, Ol' Henry knows about Kaskaskia and the big earthquake. Can you imagine the feat of the folks when the ground kept shaking and rolling for the next four months? No wonder they thought it was doomsday! The good part is that there were few lives lost, mainly because the Illinois Territory was new and not many people lived here.

You know what Ol' Henry thinks? I think that someday, someone, somewhere will find a letter Lucy wrote home to Virginia telling about the dreadful earthquake. It had to be so frightening that Lucy would have felt she just had to tell the relatives in Virginia about her experience.

Oh, oh, I see Jane coming with one of her great coffee cakes. I gotta' go — I don't want to miss a single crumb!

Se ya' later,
Henry

THE DEVELOPMENT OF THE LAND OFFICE

June 1, 2005

Life at "my" house is full of surprises with people coming and going as they continue to work. The garden committee is working hard, and it shows. The tall plant with white blooms that you can see from the street is valeriam, the "all-healing herb." Many heirloom vegetable seeds have been planted in the garden. Heirloom seeds are actually from the plants Thomas Jefferson developed at Monticello! The gardeners meet on Wednesdays, and recently they created a beautiful formal garden with boxwood plantings and four wonderful old-fashioned rose bushes. Chuck donated these exceptional plants from his nursery. Thank you, Chuck!

Ol' Henry has been hearing about a new "dig." Sid and students from SIUE have opened an excavation site in search of Col. Ben's office. So far they have not found remains of an office, but once again they have found a rubbish pile! The pile has already produced many artifacts dating back to the 1800s when Ben and Lucy were living there, including large pieces of crockery, coins, and a boot heel made with square nails!

Are you thinking: "What, another rubbish pile?" Well, remember sanitation was not a big thing in those days. So it appears there were several ways to handle trash and garbage. Any leftover food scraps were probably fed to the domestic animals. And broken, unusable items apparently were simply tossed in the rubbish pile or into the privy. Even this mouse thinks these rubbish piles were situated very close to the house.

Hey, the other day Henry here overheard George

and Sid talking about government land offices. And by golly, Ol' Henry learned a lot about what led to the formation of the government land offices and how land was acquired. Henry always knew that Col. Ben was the first to hold the prestigious position of receiver of moneys at the Edwardsville Land Office, but for whatever reason the whole picture was not clear.

The sale of federal land had its beginnings after the Revolutionary War and the creation of an American government with a national policy of expansion to the western lands that began with the Ordinance of 1787. This was the original law for the formation of new territories and states. The United States intended to take possession of the continent by whatever means possible.

This national expansion policy was included in the ratification of the U.S. Constitution. When the thirteen states signed the Constitution, they agreed to a new federal government and at the same time gave up their claims to their western lands. The first land given up by some of the states became the Northwest Territory in 1787. Within the next fifteen years, other states gave up land that later became Kentucky, Tennessee, Alabama, and Mississippi. By 1800, the ownership of all this land was in the hands of the federal government.

Ol' Henry's ears really perked up on hearing about the ownership of these lands! Why would the states give their land to the federal government? Well, the new government had no source of income. There were no federal taxes to run the government, no personal taxes, and not even business taxes. The governments of the thirteen states had been financing the federal government. The states could stop financing the federal government because of the revenue gained from selling land on the frontier. It was a darn good plan because the land sales provided enough money to run the federal government for the next one hundred years without other important taxes levied on the American people.

The Continental Congress created a plan for the new territories and states that developed from the land sales. Ol' Henry found two policies in this plan real interesting. First, it was established that a governor be appointed for each new territory, and secondly, the governor would be responsible for provisions for a militia to maintain order and protect the settlers moving into the new western frontier. Now Ol' Henry understands why Territorial Governor Ninian Edwards began the Illinois Militia when he arrived in 1809 and why Fort Russell was built. He was directed to do so by the federal government!

By 1800, the federal government had developed a consistent land-measuring system so it could start selling the land. As the government spent ten years developing its measuring system for land sales, the private land speculators had been busy. They set up their own offices and bought bounty land warrants from the Revolutionary War veterans. Ol' Henry has learned that the Revolutionary War soldiers had been paid with a certificate called a bounty land warrant for land "out west somewhere." The certificates had a set value of $1.25 an acre, but to use it the soldier had to travel to the western wilderness and claim his piece of land. These soldiers also knew that they had hostile Indians to deal with in the West, and many were not using them. A guy named Rufus Putnam ended up owning 7 million acres of the Northwest Territory at eight cents an acre!

The formation of the government land offices coincided with the development of the land measuring system in 1800, and dozens of offices were opened over the next one hundred years. George said each new land office was located at the edge of the frontier, as close as possible to the land being sold. Ol' Henry has been telling you all along that Edwardsville was the place to be. Its land office was the northernmost in the Illinois

Territory and a "jumping off" spot for young men eager to find new horizons.

These land offices showed the routes the American people took west, and roads of all sizes were built along these routes. George said that the creation of the land offices and the land sales in the State of Ohio and the Territories of Indiana, Michigan, and Illinois led to the construction of the National Road in 1815. The National Road was almost the same as the present-day U.S. Highway 40 from Baltimore to St. Louis.

So, the stories Ol' Henry heard before about Ninian Edwards and Col. Ben now fall into place. Before 1800, those who wanted to go to the western frontier gathered at the frontier's edge to wait for the territories to be opened. Edwards and Col. Ben waited at Russellville, Kentucky, where they bought land and mingled with the politicians as they strove to insure their place in the new Illinois Territory.

By 1816, the Illinois Territory land survey was completed. In April 1816, President James Madison appointed Col. Ben receiver of moneys at the Edwardsville Land Office. In October 1816, Col. Ben came from Kaskaskia to Edwardsville for the opening of the new office.

The Edwardsville Land Office was extremely busy. During the five years Col. Ben was receiver, there were 3,500 individual land sales with a total value of $900,000! As receiver of moneys, Col. Ben received a yearly salary of $1,000. In addition, he received 1 percent commission on the land sales in his office. It looks to Henry that 1 percent of $900,000 was a lot of money! Well, it looked that way to the federal government too because it soon set the commission limit at $3,000 a year!

Sid and Karen agree that the Land Office was located somewhere on Main Street in 1816, probably in Col. Ben's first house. Robert Pogue built his store in

1819 right next to Col. Ben's home, and soon the Land Office was in this new building.

Col. Ben had a prestigious, well-paid position, but Ol' Henry thinks a lot of candles were burned in the wee hours of the morning for Col. Ben to write required reports. It was not an easy job! Sid located some of the letters between Col. Ben and Josiah Meigs, head of the General Land Office in Washington, which give an idea of some of the problems encountered.

The Land Office opened in late 1816, and within three months Meigs wrote saying that the reports were arriving "considerably damaged" and asked Col. Ben ". . . instead of making them in the form of a long roll, attach the sheets together in book form . . ." and use better envelopes. In October 1817, Meigs asked that the documents be well wrapped in paper, tied and put into a cover of leather or undressed skins with the fur outside." It took months for the reports to get to Washington!

Two months later, Josiah Meigs wrote to Col. Ben: "You may think it an extraordinary fact, but so it is, that I do not know where Edwardsville is—Will you tell me the Section, Township and Range?" Well, that says a lot! The men in Washington had no clue where Edwardsville was, and they certainly had little appreciation of the conditions the Land Office faced at the edge of the western frontier. As you can imagine, the distance between Washington and Edwardsville continued to keep Col. Ben and Land Office Registrar John McKee very busy!

This has been a very long story, and Henry hopes you hung in there with me in my attempt to explain the Land Office. My hope is that you now have a better idea as to what the land offices meant to the entire United States, Edwardsville, and Col. Ben.

See ya',
Henry

A DIRECTOR, A DIG, AND A DEED

July 13, 2005

Ol' Henry heard some real good news. The Stephenson House now has a director! The Board spent several months in the director search and has chosen RoxAnn as the director of the Stephenson House. RoxAnn is a gregarious, talented, happy, and personable young woman who was site director at Ft. Madison, Iowa. She will be a terrific asset to the Stephenson House. RoxAnn is experienced and knowledgeable in many areas including period dress, docent training, educational programming, and grant writing. Ol' Henry thinks there are some really great times ahead under RoxAnn's leadership. Welcome to the Col. Benjamin Stephenson House, RoxAnn! (And, please remember to drop a few crumbs of food for me occasionally!)

By the way, Henry now has the lowdown on Sid's excavation at "my" house. The Stephenson House probate records show payment due for work on an office at Col. Ben's house. Also, there were indications that there had been a structure on the north side of the house. So, it was decided to do an excavation, in hopes of finding the office on the grounds.

Sid, our resident retired SIUE anthropology professor, led a group of students in a scientific excavation. A grid of five-foot square excavation sites was plotted out, and the students began digging in six-inch layers. Henry heard lots of giggles and chuckles as the first six-inch layer revealed tab tops, broken plastic, and paper clips. As the students dug deeper, Ol' Henry heard sounds like "Ohhhh!" "Wow!" and "Look at this!" The digging began to produce good results!

OK, what did they find? Many, many artifacts were found that provide more needed insight into the lifestyle of the Stephensons. However, there was no evidence of the office that Sid had hoped to find. The office that was mentioned in the probate records probably was located at Col. Ben's first brick house on N. Main Street, across from the first public square. Today, this area is a parking lot.

The structure to the north of the house ended up being a waste dump. This was the biggest dump of all, and many things of interest were found. This dump was started in 1820 and continued until perhaps 1900. The location of the dump makes it seem that what was broken or not needed was simply tossed out the kitchen window into the dump! Remember, it was 1820 and 1830! The sight of Lucy or an indentured servant tossing trash out the kitchen window makes Ol' Henry smile!

The oldest items identified so far are two buttons worn on clothing from the 1790s. That is pretty darn old, and a good guess is that the buttons are from a shirt someone brought with them to the Illinois Territory.

Fragments of green featherware plates, bowls, and cups were found. Remember, Sid found blue transferware and blue featherware fragments in the privy excavation. It looks like the Stephensons had three sets of dishes that were very popular in the early 1800s. Also, an 1821 George IV coronation coin with a hole drilled at the top was found. Maybe the coin had been made into a necklace for Lucy!

The long list of items also includes clay marbles, glass marbles, pieces of six or seven clay pipes, a brass locket with a glass bead on the edges, and mocha ware. Mocha ware dishes were used by the middle class and often used in taverns. Ummmm, wonder why Col. Ben had mocha ware?

Again, a lot of bottles were found with perhaps half being from the Stephenson time period and the other half from the Wolf family. Crockery chards, made of clay with a dark glaze and etchings, had been tossed in the dump.

Let me tell you about THE greatest find of all in the excavation: A ham bone with serious mouse teeth marks! Yep, it was in with other artifacts that date from when Col. Ben and Lucy lived here. Ol' Henry just knows that it was great-great-great grandfather Samuel who spent a lot of time with that ham bone! That old guy always did tell the young ones to nibble around on bones to get the calcium they needed. Hey, it's about time those archaeologists started looking for my Stephenson mouse ancestors!!

Soon, the dig will be finished, and then the task of sorting, labeling, and organizing all the artifacts will begin. Ol' Henry peeked into the containers and could see there were a lot of bags full of "stuff" to organize! Hey, be sure and check out the artifacts on display. Once again, the Stephenson House has benefited by people who care and are interested in preserving the past. A big thanks to Sid and the students!

The researchers continued to be busy too! They have new information, and it must be good. They sure are smiling big smiles! They have located deeds for land Col. Ben and Lucy purchased. A land deed includes lots of information the researchers need, such as the date, name of buyer or seller, the county and state where they live, in addition to a description of the land and purchase price. No wonder Karen and that bunch are happy!

Ol' Henry heard long ago that Col. Ben and Lucy lived in Harper's Ferry, Virginia, in 1803, when their first child Julia was born. These newly found land deeds prove that the Stephensons lived in Jefferson County, Virginia, around 1803. I hear there are a number of

Stephenson deeds for property in Jefferson County with the last one dated May 1806.

Col. Ben and Lucy were on the move, and by August 1806—maybe as early as March—they were living in the Wellsburg area in Brooke County, Virginia. They had good reason to be there because Lucy was of age to inherit from her father's estate. It looks like Col. Ben and Lucy, daughter Julia, and newborn son James lived in Brooke County while the estate was being settled. Ben Stephenson even served as a juror on three juries in Brooke County in August 1806. Ol' Henry knows Karen wishes there were more details about the settlement of the estate of Lucy's father "Indian" Van. The estate settlement records do show that in August 1806 Col. Ben and Lucy sold a parcel of the Brooke County land she had inherited. Col. Ben and Lucy sold 150 acres in Brooke County for $3,000!

Well, the researchers continued searching for the trail of the Stephenson family before they came to Illinois in 1809. A deed for land the Stephensons sold in 1807 shows Col. Ben and Lucy living in Logan County, Kentucky. The Stephensons were still living there in March 1809, when their daughter Elvira was born.

The other day, Ol' Henry was hanging out in great-great grandpappy Ezra's great hidey place when Karen came with good news to share with Sid. The researchers have finally been able to pinpoint an actual area where Col. Ben and Lucy lived before they came to Illinois. Yep, a Logan County, Kentucky, deed for land sold by Ben and Lucy in August 1809 states that the Stephensons lived on a thousand acres of land located "on the waters of the Whipperwill." It was time to get a map of Kentucky and find the Whipperwill! Sure enough, Ol' Henry was there when they located the Whipperwill River in Logan County, Kentucky. The river runs south from Russellville to Tennessee.

Remember, we knew Benjamin Stephenson was a charter member of the Free and Accepted Masons in Russellville. Now we know where the Stephensons lived in Russellville. This mouse knows the researchers are very excited and happy with their findings! They have searched a long time as they tried to figure out where Ben and Lucy were before they came to Illinois. Finally, they have been successful and as one said, they sure hope this is just the tip of the iceberg! Henry has all his fingers and toes crossed for you!

See ya' later,
Henry

126 *Henry's Diary*

WHAT'S COOKING AND GROWING AROUND THE HOUSE!

August 10, 2005

Hi! Henry the Stephenson House mouse is back again. Well, a lot of projects have been completed around here within the last few months. And, there is a big new one starting, the summer kitchen! Sure 'nuff, the construction of the summer kitchen has already begun. Ol' Henry was happy to see Keith and Jack return here to work. I sure missed them! The kitchen is already taking shape as the two guys work away.

Henry listened when Joe and Sid talked with Jamie and Lynn about the plans for the summer kitchen being built to the south of the porch. It will be a two-story brick building with a big hearth and a brick beehive oven. Now, Ol' Henry knows a hearth contains a cooking fire over which the family meals were cooked. But, a beehive oven was used for baking bread and other goodies and is different looking. Ol' Henry can't figure out how to describe this oven to you; I am just a mouse ya' know! So, it will be a nice surprise for you all to come see later. Henry does know for sure that this summer kitchen is really going to be a cool building! It will be furnished with a table and chairs, workspace, and early cooking utensils. The second floor will be like the sparsely furnished living space that had been used by the Stephensons' indentured servants.

The summer kitchen is a very important part of the Stephenson House, as it will be used for many educational and fun programs for all ages. RoxAnn, the director, will probably begin with programs for the younger kids and work up to projects for big people.

There is a lot of fun ahead!

Ol' Henry has been "sitting in" on the classes at the archaeological dig as I try to get educated! It sure is fun to watch and learn as "new" artifacts are found. Just the other day a token was found in the dig that presented a question Sid would like answered. The token has printed on it: "good for 5 cents in Decker's Café." If you know anything about a place called Decker's Café, please call Sid. Sid would really like to know the years when Decker's Café was in business. If Sid could find the date of Decker's Café, it would help him in dating other artifacts found. This dig has been fun for all of us and has educated Henry!

Hey, Cousin Jake came by the other day! The news of "my" great garden has reached Lower Town and Jake came to take a look. So, Ol' Henry gave Cousin Jake a tasting tour of the garden! We both like the sunflower seeds, and Ol' Henry knew from listening to Carol F. that these sunflowers with a red center are a rare variety. The yellow finch really like these seeds too! Jake and Henry also sampled the tasty sesame seeds. The seeds planted in "my" garden were harvested from sesame plants that a man named Thomas Jefferson planted in his kitchen garden long ago. He had planted sesame in order to press a salad oil from the seeds. Hmmmm, smart guy!

Ol' Henry heard Carol F. say that Jefferson had planted lots of seeds at his home, which is called Monticello. Seeds harvested from Jefferson's Monticello gardens are still available, and Carol F. has used many in "my" garden. The green peppers are also from seeds at Monticello, and Henry and Jake know for sure that these peppers are juicy, sweet, and tender. And there are lots of them left! A clove-like flower called Globe Amaranth was planted by Jefferson on April 2, 1767, at his boyhood home, a place called

Shadewell. This Globe Amaranth is blooming right now with magenta and pink flowers, which will last a long time. One of the gardeners said these are also called straw flowers.

Then Cousin Jake and I tasted the tomatoes! Carol F. and her group planted several kinds of old-fashioned, like those from the 1800s, tomatoes. Some are little and red, and some yellow and pear shaped. There are tomatoes with names like Brandywine, Arkansas Traveller, Burbank, and Red Calabash. Sid says the Red Calabash tomatoes are the sweetest of all. Let's just say Cousin Jake and Henry liked all of them a whole lot!

There is also wild flax planted in the garden. Henry learned from listening to Carol F. that this wild flax was discovered by men named Lewis and Clark a long, long time ago. This flower doesn't taste real good, but it sure is pretty! Cousin Jake and Henry loved the garden, and we found a lot of things we really liked to eat. We are now waiting to see what the gardeners plant for fall!

All this talk about the garden has made this guy real hungry. Ol' Henry is going to scamper over to the garden and get some sesame seeds to go with the cheese I have hidden away!

See ya' later,
Henry

THE FOURTH OF JULY

October 26, 2005

These last weeks remind Ol' Henry of the summer not so long ago when E. J., Keith, and Jack reinforced the old second floor joists that the monster termites enjoyed many years ago. Well, it was hot! One of the guys wrote the temp (103 degrees) and date on one of the new joists. Now, just how hot do you think it has been as Keith and Jack work on the summer kitchen? Ol' Henry thinks it has been hotter than 103 — probably more like 109! I sure am glad that Keith's wife has kept them supplied with water!

Hey, how about that summer kitchen? Since it is new construction, some of the rules of restoration do not apply, and concrete blocks are being used for the frame. The summer kitchen is going to really look great and a big thank you to Kienstra, Inc. for the concrete blocks and to Richards Brick, our favorite brick company, who donated the bricks for the exterior walls. You are both wonderful friends! Just squint your eyes and picture the completed building with brick walls and a shake roof! Nice, huh?

The word summer kitchen means different things to different people. It could be the outside kitchen folks used during the hot months of summer to keep the cooking heat away from the living quarters. It also could be the kitchen detached from the house for year-round use. We know the Stephensons had an attached kitchen, but there is a good chance they also had a kitchen for summer use. So, the building is authentic to the time period.

Col. Ben's house has been restored as much to the original as possible, but there are a few modern wonders! There is a bathroom, running water, electric lights in some areas, a telephone, and a computer! The Stephenson House telephone number is 692-1818, and the email is stephensonhouse@sbc.net. You are welcome to telephone or e-mail for answers to any questions you may have.

Henry here has been lying back in the shade, staying real still, wishing for a breeze and just reminiscing. Got to thinking about how Col. Ben celebrated on the Fourth of July. Why did Ol' Henry think of the Fourth of July? Probably because it is so hot! And, Col. Ben loved the day! The stories the great-great grandpappies Samuel and Ezra told about the big celebrations on the Fourth of July in Kaskaskia and in Edwardsville are still remembered.

How did they celebrate the Fourth of July when the United States was so young? In 1810, the men met under an arbor in Kaskaskia for dinner in the afternoon. After dinner they made toasts in celebration of the colonies' independence. They made toasts, drank to toasts, made more toasts, and drank to more toasts. Each toast was followed with the firing of volleys. Toasts were held high for George Washington, President James Madison, Liberty, the Constitution, the vice president, Congress, the heroes of '76, the militia, industry, and the economy! A St. Louis newspaper reported a toast to the demise of the bad guys Benedict Arnold, Aaron Burr, and their associates: "May every traitor like them, fall before the strong hand of American indignation." The patriotic fever was high!

Our friend Rose found information about the celebration in Kaskaskia in 1810 in an old St. Louis newspaper. It reported: "The utmost harmony prevailed throughout the day . . . the celebration of the day was closed by an elegant ball in the evening at Major B. Stephenson's, where a brilliant circle of Ladies attended . . ." Col. Ben made sure the ladies also celebrated the Fourth of July!

All the Stephenson House mouse families know the stories told about the Fourth of July in 1819 in Edwardsville. Col. Ben presided over the activities of the day, and probate records show that he spent a good deal of money on the celebration. Old Ezra would smile real big as he told how the day began at noon with a procession that walked from the Edwardsville Hotel to Daniel Tolman's new building, where a full day of speeches began. Gen. R. Hopkins, an old Revolutionary War survivor, read the Declaration of Independence, an oration was made by Nicholas Hansen, and by midafternoon it was time for the excellent dinner prepared by W. C. Wiggins, the popular innkeeper.

Of course, many toasts followed the meal. Cheers followed each toast, and the number of cheers was recorded. Old Ezra's story relates that most toasts got three cheers; some got six cheers, and one got nine cheers. Only two toasts received twelve cheers! One was the toast made "to the degraded and unfortunate sons of Africa. May man soon cease to dishonor his Maker and disgrace himself by trafficking in human flesh." The other toast to receive twelve cheers was the toast to the State of Illinois with its wise constitution, healthful climate, fertile soil, diversified woods, and prairie making it the most desirable of the new states!

Apparently some of the men had their toasts prepared before the day. Daniel Smith toasted with a poem that Ezra said went like this: "A comet appeared last night in the sky, To give us a toast for the Fourth of July: May she sail up Missouri, and—slavery—end it, And scorch with her tail those that wish to extend it."

The Fourth of July celebration of 1819 was very different from our celebrations today. When was the last time you heard the Declaration of Independence read aloud?

See ya' later,
Henry

1820s SOCIALIZING

October 26, 2005

This has been a great time to just hang around, hang out, and watch the people come and go. RoxAnn and the new volunteer Erin have put the volunteer and docent program into high gear, starting with training sessions in November. The volunteers will learn about the early history of the Illinois Territory, the county, and the Stephenson House. They will learn about period clothing, period speaking, and they will observe a sample tour of the Stephenson House. Long ago Ol' Henry said he would let you know when you were needed. Well, this is the call from Henry.

Keith has finished all the brickwork on the kitchen, including the beehive oven on the east outside wall. It is so cool! Now Keith and Jack are working to finish the roof, the interior floor, and the staircase. When done, the kitchen will be ready. The other day, Ol' Henry looked out from his hidey place and saw smoke coming from the kitchen chimney! Keith was checking out his handy work, and yes, the kitchen fireplace does work! Next thing you know, RoxAnn will be cooking in the kitchen. Henry can't wait for that to happen!

Did you see the super cornstalk wrapped around the lamppost? Henry heard that Jill grows this kind of stuff for decoration, and she gave this one to the Stephenson House. Thanks Jill! Henry loves it 'cause it is a good place to play and watch the world go by. One sunny morning, Ol' Henry was peeping out from the cornstalks at the cars going by and got to thinking about where all those people were going. Did the folks in 1818, 1820, and 1822 do anything except work? Each day had to be filled, considering the time it took to grow and cook food, bake bread, take care of the animals, make soap and candles, and chop wood needed for cooking and heating fires!

Henry here just knew that these folks had to get together and do some fun things! Finally, I started remembering the stories great-great grandpappy Ezra told about how Edwardsville residents started different societies as a way to advance their interests and to socialize. Henry here remembers what Old Ezra told about the physicians who formed a medical association. He said John Todd was the first president, and the First District Medical Society of the State of Illinois met in Edwardsville in May 1820. At the same time, the mechanics formed an organization known as the Edwardsville Mechanics Society. A singing society was also organized around this time, and the first public library in Illinois was formed right here in Edwardsville. The librarian was John Randall, and Benaiah Robinson, the surveyor, was on the board of directors. Great-great grandpappy Ezra spoke about an annual meeting of the stockholders of the Edwardsville Library in January 1821. The meeting was held at the courthouse where they elected five directors. This was the first courthouse, and it was a log cabin built in the Public Square.

There was a Female Sunday School Society in Edwardsville in the early 1820s. Old Ezra said that Lucy was secretary of this society, and he heard her say there were two schools that met each Sunday. One was for "colored people" who attended regularly and were happy with the instruction. Lucy said the second school was for people of her race, and it was intended to correct the morals of those who, by a series of oppressions, had been lowered to ignorance and vice. The society felt that only the greatest moral instruction could help them. Old Ezra said it appeared that the society felt real strong about the Sunday School Society and even opened it to men. Looks like the women decided the men could use some help too!

All the societies had a cause and a reason for being formed, but Henry knows there was the social side of each group, and the members had a good time.

The residents in the 1820s were not without entertainment. For example, the St. Louis Theatrical Corps performed dramatic theatre at the home of John and Lucretia Lusk. This took place on a Tuesday, Wednesday, and Thursday evening in May 1820.

In September 1820, Gov. Shadrach Bond reviewed the regiment of militia under the command of Col. William Parkinson. This was a special day with lots of activities for everyone.

The story Ol' Henry remembers best is about the Museum of Fine Arts that came to Edwardsville. This exhibit had it all, including a variety of paintings and imitations of life in wax. There was also a powerful electric machine and apparatus to be observed. And, there was music on an elegant organ and more! The exhibition was held during the first week of court, and admission was twenty-five cents and kids half price.

So much for the bit of early Edwardsville culture for now, because this old mouse is going to take one more scamper through the garden. The gardeners are ready to put the garden to bed for the winter, and Ol' Henry needs to make sure all the seeds have been gathered up for my winter meals!

See ya' later,
Henry

FRONTIER JUSTICE IN MADISON

November 9, 2005

Hi! Henry the Stephenson House mouse is back again, keeping an eye on the preparations for the March opening of the Stephenson House, and believe me, there is a lot going on. Right now there are day and evening training sessions for volunteer docents. Henry is learning too, as I listen from my hidey place. I hear them say that the house is always looking for volunteers!

How about that kitchen? Keith and Jack have the shake roof completed and are now working on the inside. The other day Ol' Henry heard Keith moving around in the kitchen way before the sun was up. That was kinda' early so Henry went back to sleep. Later in the day good smells were coming from the kitchen. Ol' Henry twitched his nose and perked up his ears to find out what was going on. Turns out Keith can cook, and he was making ham and beans for dinner! He had soaked the beans before the sun came up until mid-morning. Then he added leeks and ham hocks and hung the big black iron pot over the fire in the kitchen fireplace. A few hours later, Keith took the pot off the fire and just sat it on the hearth where heat in the bricks continued to cook the beans. At dinnertime, the beans were steaming hot and fit for a king. Ol' Henry sure enjoyed the beans that I know Keith left for me. Thanks Keith!

A few days ago, Henry here packed a lunch and headed to visit Cousin Jake in Lower Town. When Ol' Henry arrived he found Cousin Jake and his buddies sharing a big bag of corn chips. It sure was good to see everyone again, and better yet, corn chips are Henry's favorite snack!

It turns out they were talking about the punishment for fighting and stealing in Edwardsville around 1820. At that time, the State of Illinois was brand new, but Madison County already had a court, judges, and juries to decide on punishments and fines.

Hey, Cousin Jake and his buddies told about the court ordering a man found guilty of stealing to receive thirty-one lashes on the bare back, well laid on, at the public square in Edwardsville! This ruling was punishment for stealing thirteen dollars worth of clothing and a book, and get this, all of the stuff had been returned to the owner except for a five-dollar pair of pantaloons. Well, the guys gave Ol' Henry a hard time when they realized I did not know that this kind of punishment ever happened in Edwardsville. Ol' Henry had just never, ever heard these stories! Gosh, Ol' Henry had always thought the worst thing that had happened at the public square was the trial of Edward Coles about his freeing of his slaves.

The same term of court in 1820 tried two men for stealing $1,050 worth of U.S. notes, watches, compasses, magnets, and magnifying glasses. The watches and money were returned to the owners. The court ordered the two thieves to receive thirty-one lashes, on the bare back, and also well laid on. Henry was shocked!

You know, this old mouse does wonder how the court decided thirty-one lashes for a theft of thirteen dollars, and also thirty-one lashes for a theft of $1,050.

Cousin Jake had a few more stories to tell about different punishments for stealing. On the same day, Jacob Stump received twenty-five lashes for stealing, and Charles, a black man, was sentenced to thirty-five lashes for stealing. Later, the court reconsidered the case of Charles and increased his sentence to forty lashes. My gosh!

Sure looks to Henry that stealing was not to be tolerated, probably because of the high value given to property rights. A lot of lashes on the bare back and well laid on should make a thief think twice before he stole. Henry learned a lot about the people and the law in 1820 Edwardsville.

Fighting, also called riot and assault and battery, brought a lot of men to court. Cousin Jake's buddies chuckled when they told Ol' Henry that Hail Mason, a justice of the peace; Theophilus Smith, a judge; and David Gillespie, father of Judge Joseph Gillespie, were all charged with fighting! They knew these men were friends of Col. Ben and loved to tell Ol' Henry the stories. Ol' Henry was embarrassed about how much he did not know. There sure must have been a lot of fighting going on in Edwardsville. When Theophilus Smith was charged, he was one of thirty-nine men who were fighting. Wonder if it was the same fight? Well, at least they were not killing each other!

Henry here did ask what the punishment was for fighting. Could Theophilus Smith possibly have received lashes for fighting? No. Cousin Jake made it clear that the usual fine for fighting was three dollars, but sometimes the fine would be as high as twenty-five, fifty, or even one hundred dollars. Jake said that Theophilus let the judge decide his fate, rather than a jury, and he got off with a fine of twelve cents.

Cousin Jake's buddies were really having a great time telling Ol' Henry about who got into trouble in 1820! They had to tell me about William May, a friend of Col. Ben's, who was charged for burglary, and Jeptha Lampkin who was charged with kidnapping. Who in the world would a man kidnap in 1820 in Edwardsville?

Well, it sure was some visit with Cousin Jake and his buddies. Ol' Henry certainly learned a lot and did a lot of thinking on the trip back home. One thing is for sure, 1820 was many, many years ago, and life was really different in Edwardsville.

See ya' later,
Henry

COL. BEN AND THE COURTHOUSE

February 15, 2006

Hi! Henry the Stephenson House mouse is back again. Brrrrrrrrr, the cold winter weather has arrived but it sure doesn't slow down activity at the Stephenson House! Keith and Jack are busy with several projects that will give neat finishing touches to the grounds. They are building an old-fashioned flagpole that is really cool. And, they are erecting a corner of the brick foundation of Col. Ben's barn so folks will be able to actually see the many courses of brick used in the foundation. Ol' Henry thinks it is great having the privy, kitchen, vegetable garden, and now the barn area identified. Even Henry has a better idea of how the grounds of "my" house looked when great-great-great grandpappy Samuel came to live here with Col. Ben and Lucy and the kids lots of years ago.

Volunteers are preparing to guide house tours and RoxAnn and others are busy sewing period clothing for the volunteers. RoxAnn and Erin are looking for more volunteers for a multitude of things, including sewing easy period dresses for the volunteers. A volunteer group of people playing cards will make the dining room come alive. A woman doing needlework or just reading a book will add charm to any room. Volunteer men and women are needed in the kitchen to demonstrate cooking over an open fire. Join up! You can pretty well pick your own hours!! You all be sure to come visit soon! Ol' Henry will be excited to see you!

The bedrooms are looking absolutely awesome! George and Elizabeth made tickings stuffed with hay for "mattresses" just as they used in 1820. It was a big job stuffing all that hay into the tickings, but they had fun! Kathy made beautiful hangings for the four-poster bed in the master bedroom. Ol' Henry thinks the top part is called a canopy with long, curtain-like hangings on the posters. Henry thinks they were closed around the bed for warmth in the winter. The bedroom looks like it did long, long ago and is beautiful!

During the past few years, Ol' Henry has heard a lot of stories about the people and events of early Edwardsville that I kinda' stored away to think about later. One of the stories concerns Col. Ben, Theopolis Smith, Ninian Edwards, and others and their offer to donate the land and materials for the construction of a Madison County courthouse and jail at their own expense. Sounds like a pretty good deal for the county, right? Well, Ol' Henry asked Cousin Jake and the guys in Lower Town to tell me what they knew about this story. Sure enough, they knew all about it.

Cousin Jake told me that Col. Ben and friends also offered to donate fifty town lots that the county could then sell for income to maintain the courthouse and jail. The only condition was that the courthouse and jail be erected in the southeastern part of Edwardsville. This was an area called Upper Edwardsville, nicknamed "Buncomb."

Well, let this mouse tell you that when word of this offer hit the streets of Edwardsville in early 1820, it really started a rumble in Lower Town. These people did not want the courthouse to leave the public square in Lower Town or "old town."

The Lower Town guys let Ol' Henry know real quickly what the problem was with Col. Ben's proposal. In 1820, Upper Edwardsville contained only a few houses, and its residents were wealthy, if not aristocratic. The people from Lower Town resented that Upper Edwardsville money was trying to move the courthouse from the public square.

Immediately following Col. Ben's proposal, the opposition in Lower Town made a counter-proposal to the county commissioners for what eventually became known as "The Donation Courthouse." About twenty-five citizens of Edwardsville made this counter-proposal that stated what each individual would donate in cash or materials to erect a courthouse on the public square. They would erect the building and donate it to Madison County. The amount of their intended donations totaled about $2,500.

The honorable county commissioners, Samuel Judy, George Barnsback, and William Jones, now had two proposals to choose from for the construction of the courthouse and jail, and they were unable to make a decision. Cousin Jake and his buddies said Commissioner Jones was not friendly to Edwardsville, but many people were very curious why Barnsback and Judy hesitated to accept one of the two offers. Anyway, the matter was deferred until after the county election in August.

Maybe some of you know the rest of the story! The new county commissioners—Amos Squire, James Tunnell, and Abraham Prickett—were friends with Col. Ben's opponents, and the commissioners jumped on this counter-proposal and invited bids for contracts at once. Among the bidders were Jeptha Lamkin $5,000, Walter Seeley $2,800, Benjamin Stephenson $2,000, T. W. Smith $1,500, and Hooper Warren $200. Apparently, the county had advertised it would take the low bid. Ninian Edwards bid $100, stating that he would erect the jail at the place advertised, within the time frame and according to advertised plans for the jail. Ninian's bid was rejected, and Ol' Henry wonders about Ninian's reaction!

The bid was awarded to Walter Seeley, and he erected the jail and met all the specifications of his contract with the county. However, Seeley's experience with the county was not good. In 1822, he wrote to the commissioners of the county stating that he now had debts he could not pay because he had furnished materials for the jail. He pleaded for the county to pay him. Apparently, the county had not paid him any money. Seeley was ill and confined, and the constable was at his door ready to sell Seeley's own property in payment for the jail debts. The court ordered this letter filed, and it remained filed until sixty years later when it was found. Cousin Jake and his buddies did not know if Seeley ever got paid or if the constable sold his property to pay his debts.

Remember Stephenson and Smith's proposal included a courthouse. Well, guys, in 1821 the county court also accepted a proposal by John York Sawyer and others for the building of a brick courthouse on the public square. The group of twenty-five citizens who made the proposal would pay for the "Donation Courthouse" in either cash or materials. The building progressed very slowly, even with prodding from the court. Finally, in 1825, the court released J. T. Lusk, Paris Mason, and Joshua Atwater from their bond to erect the courthouse. They were to just finish off the dirt floor and get all materials intended for the courthouse to the county so the circuit court could meet there on the next Monday. Between 1831 and 1835, the courthouse was completed at public expense, enabled by raiding the school fund. Formal possession of the courthouse took place on June 25, 1835. The guys in Lower Town remember hearing stories how the new "Donation Courthouse" was pitiful and certainly not much of an improvement over the first log cabin courthouse.

Cousin Jake told this story: An eccentric evangelist, Lorenzo Dow, came to town to preach and was shown the courthouse as the meeting place. He refused to preach there, saying, "It is only fit for a hog pen." The floor was dirt, and there were no stairs to reach the second floor. The old men serving as jurors had to climb a steep and fragile ladder to reach the upper floor. This courthouse served Madison County until 1857. Ol' Henry sure hopes there were some improvements made between 1835 and 1857. Golly, what a poor decision it was to turn down the offer made by Stephenson, Smith, Edwards, and others for a new courthouse and jail!

See ya' later,
Henry

TOOLS, GRIKES, AND FENCES

March 29, 2006

Long ago, Ol' Henry heard a lady say, "It's the little things that make a house a home," and now this mouse understands what she meant. She meant the little things like the clothes rack with wooden pegs that Jim C. hung in the quarters above the kitchen and the hanging rack that Bob W. made from an antique rake. Jim C. put the hanging rack in the kitchen where it now holds wooden cooking implements. Hey, "my" house is looking like a home!

The big surprise for Ol' Henry the other day was when I was looking around the parlor and saw a beautiful color portrait of Col. Ben above the mantel! Later, Henry learned that this portrait was a wonderful gift to the Stephenson House from the Madison County Family Physicians. What a great gift, and a big thanks to all the physicians from all of us at the Stephenson House, including Henry. St. Louis artist Lon Brauer, who is RoxAnn's friend, painted this reproduction from a photo of the 1800 watercolor on ivory miniature of Col. Ben that is in the Smithsonian American Art Museum. The portrait is beautiful and really helps make "my" house a home! Be sure and come see for yourself!

This old mouse wants you to know that some mighty good down-home cooking has been going on here. A few days ago, Vickie and Dixie, RoxAnn's friends, cooked a great meal of fresh bread, stew, and apple crisp baked in the open hearth in a large Dutch oven. And, Dixie made butter and whipped cream for the finishing touch! Ol' Henry wonders if the word about all this good food has reached Cousin Jake and his buddies in Lower Town.

You know, Henry hangs pretty close to Keith and Jack 'cause they are fun and always busy! Their latest project is fences! Here they were, working hard finishing the authentic 1820 Stephenson picket fence around the shade garden, and the next thing Ol' Henry sees is a split-rail fence going up by the grape arbor! From what I hear this is a sample split-rail fence to help the Friends decide about fencing around the property. Looks good to Henry.

The Paint Crew is finished with painting projects, and they are now officially known as the Tuesday Morning Crew. They are a super bunch of guys who help with cleaning, sweeping, preparing the shade garden, and doing other odd jobs. The Tuesday Morning Crew is a tremendous asset to the Stephenson House. They have fun and good ideas and keep things spruced up at "my" house. They simply do whatever needs to be done and have fun doing it! Ol' Henry sees a lot from his hidey place and knows these guys are great!

One day Henry heard the guys of the Tuesday Morning Crew talk about the amount of hard physical labor needed to survive in the early 1800s. Joe mentioned the hand-hewn beams in Col. Ben's house and how they were made. It took a strong man! He said they used a broad or squaring axe to chip away at round logs to make them square. The broad axe was level on one side, had a short handle, and a razor sharp blade. Joe smiled as he said, "You had to be on your toes every second or the broad axes would."

Just as Ol' Henry was wondering what kept the round log from rolling around, Chuck came up with the answer. Dogs were used to clamp the log down. Dogs? Well, he said that there were a lot of things called dogs in the early days, including a lump of iron and fireplace andirons that looked like little dogs. Col.

Ben and Lucy had andiron dogs, and there are some at the fireplaces now.

There were also hewing dogs that were used to clamp down the log to be hewed. Chuck read that hewing dogs were two spikes joined by an iron bar about twenty inches long. One spike was anchored into the log and the other spike anchored into a short piece of square beam where the log rested. This kept the log from rolling around, and all the man had to worry about was his toes!

The guys talked about pit saws, the chisel axe, and fences. The fence stories interested Ol' Henry. Rail and stone fences had slits in them called "grikes." Some people believe these spaces, especially in the stone fences, were used to shoot through in Indian fighting. They were actually spaces for people to squeeze through and were small enough that the farm animal would be too timid to attempt to escape. The men even made little ladders called wood stiles so the women could get over the rail fences. Old Henry just loves it when the guys talk about the old days!

See ya' later,
Henry

A DEDICATION AND CELEBRATION

July 6, 2006

Hi! Henry the Stephenson House mouse is back again. The Dedication and Celebration of the Benjamin Stephenson House was this past weekend. What a weekend it turned out to be! The Dedication and Celebration was truly a celebration just like Col. Ben would have enjoyed in the 1820s. The craftspeople of the 1820s were here demonstrating their skills. The wheat weaver was making fantastic hats, while a cooper made barrels, and a militiaman created bullets in molds over a hot fire. The Windsor chair maker, the rope maker, and the herb lady were all working and enjoying the company of each other and visiting with guests.

There was period music throughout the weekend, and the Alton Fife and Drum Corp entertained folks in the porch area with a great performance. Ol' Henry enjoyed the weekend with cooking going on in the kitchen, seeing folks touring "my" house, and seeing the kids jumping rope with the rope they had made themselves with direction from the rope maker.

In recognition of Col. Ben's pride and enjoyment of the day when our nation's independence is celebrated — the Fourth of July — Carol and the committee selected the Fourth as the weekend for our Dedication and Celebration of the restoration of Col. Ben's home. You will remember that Col. Ben presided over the Fourth of July activities in 1819, and it was a very long eventful day!

Ol' Henry listened carefully to the speakers and enjoyed each one. Henry remembers Carol introducing Ben Dickmann, who gave the invocation, and Paul

Herbert, a high school student, who sang "America." Senator Bowles, Karen Mateyka, Joe Weber, Director RoxAnn, Mayor Niebur, U.S. Congressman John Shimkus, and Senator Bill Haine all made brief remarks. Ol' Henry sure was glad the speakers and the crowd did not do over forty speeches, cheers, and toasts like in the 1820s!

As you will remember, Senator Bowles was instrumental in getting the restoration started when she secured the initial grant money from the State of Illinois. In the years following, many people contributed so much in time and money to enable the completion of the restoration of Col. Ben's home. Each and every one of these people should be so proud of whatever she or he did in this great effort.

Joe Weber emphasized that the restoration was blessed with a structure that had a strong foundation on which to work. The substantial structure was the result of the hard work and quality skills of the Stephenson indentured servants. The work of Winn, Tobe, Hannah, Hark, Barksley, Caroline, Louise, Deborah, Washing Will, and Jesse produced a home that has stood for almost 200 years, a home that we can all be so very proud of.

It was goosebump time for Ol' Henry when the Fife and Drum Corp paraded to the flagpole and raised the official flag of 1820. Paul then led the crowd in the singing of "The Star Spangled Banner." What a beautiful closing of the weekend event.

Well, it was a long, hot, busy weekend for this old mouse, but I really had fun. It was a great weekend! Oh, Cousin Jake counted and there are twenty-three stars on the blue field in the 1820s flag, one for each state in the Union at that time!

See ya' later,
Henry

HENRY'S TOUR OF THE STEPHENSON HOUSE

Henry here is very proud of Col. Ben's house, and so I would like to take you on a personal tour.

THE GROUNDS

Let's start with touring the grounds and the kitchen, then we will talk about the structure of Col. Ben's house. Here on the porch is a really pleasant place to view the grounds.

The vegetable garden is in the southeast corner of the grounds, and in the growing season it is full of plants grown from seeds from the 1820s plants. The garden committee creates a productive and beautiful garden that features magnificent sunflowers and a neat scarecrow with a head made from a gourd. There are several herb gardens containing herbs original to the 1820s that were used for cooking and medicinal purposes. A lovely grape arbor is on the south side of the kitchen and will soon be producing grapes for jam and wine! Col. Ben's house was built on 182 acres, and Ol' Henry is sure the original gardens were much larger.

THE KITCHEN

Ol' Henry loves the kitchen! Tasty food is cooked on the open hearth, and bread and rolls come piping hot from the bustle or beehive oven. The original 1820 Stephenson kitchen was attached to the main house, which was unusual for that time. Today's separate kitchen is an authentic reproduction of the attached 1820s kitchen. The ghost line of the original kitchen roof is visible on the second floor.

Around 1845, the Wolf family took the kitchen down to the ground and built a new kitchen with a large second story on the original 1820 kitchen foundation.

Today, the 1845 addition houses the museum giftshop, the orientation room, and offices on the second floor.

The second floor of today's kitchen is furnished as living quarters for the Stephenson slaves or indentured servants similar to those in the original attached kitchen. From the original kitchen, there was access to the children's bedroom through a small doorway that you will see later. The roof ghost line is above this doorway.

Here is what Henry understands why Col. Ben's people were called either slaves or indentured servants. They were called slaves until the early 1800s when the legal term became indentured servants. From what Ol' Henry has learned by listening to others, the two terms pretty well mean the same thing. The difference was that slaves were the property of the owner for their lifetime, while indentured servants, although they were also property of the owner, had a date set for when they would be freed.

THE PRIVY

On the north side of the house is a reproduction of the large Stephenson privy built on the original privy site. This privy was a three-holer with a size for men, women, and children. How about that!

THE HOUSE

The Exterior
I am sure you have noticed the wonderful breeze that flows through the porch area! Folks love to sit here and enjoy the breeze that soothes even on the warmest summer days.

Now come with Henry to the front of Col. Ben's house. The house is a classic southern Federal style of architecture. Federal style is symmetrical, and therefore, each side is a mirror image of the other. There are four rooms in this two-story house with two rooms on each floor, and each room is 18' × 18' with 10' ceilings. The brick pattern is Flemish bond style. Flemish bond style means that every sixth row or course of bricks is laid with one long brick, one short end, one long brick, and one short end for the entire row. Jack Arches are at the top of the downstairs windows. In this style of arch, the bricks are cut at an angle and the design supports the upper story.

Have you noticed there are no shrubs or bushes planted near the house foundation? The folks of the 1820s knew that shrubs and vegetation attracted insects and other pests that would come into the windows!

The Interior
Foyer

Come inside with Henry for a tour of this beautifully restored 1820s home. This house is full of many antiques that are all interesting and fun to learn about. I am going to show you some of Ol' Henry's favorite things in "my" house. Please follow me through the front door. There is the beautiful staircase with its walnut handrail! The 1810 chandelier, lighted by three candles, casts a warm glow in the foyer as you look upward to the awesome window at the top of the stairs. You now realize that you are in a beautiful old home.

Parlor

Now look to our left. This is the parlor where the Stephenson family gathered. The children probably played or read, and Lucy may have passed the time doing fine needlework as Col. Ben read the latest *Spectator*. The books in the secretary are old copies of the books that Col. Ben had in his library. There are also copies of books that Col. Ben donated to the first Edwardsville library.

The portrait above the parlor fireplace is of Col. Ben, painted by artist Lon Brauer of St. Louis and was a gift from a group of local physicians. Ol' Henry loves to tell the story about the portrait! When the restoration started, the researchers started searching for more information about Col Ben. They located a picture of him in the Stephenson County Court House in Freeport, Illinois, the county that is named for him. The Freeport newspapers of 1914 reported that the picture was from a tintype done of Col. Ben when he was in Cuba, Missouri, around 1800. A copy of that very picture is in the Orientation Room right here at "my" house! A few years later, a watercolor on ivory miniature was located at the Smithsonian American Art Museum. Talk about excitement! It turned out the tintype was a copy of the miniature that is documented by the Smithsonian, but the tintype was reversed. The story of the tintype and the miniature is one Ol' Henry would love to know more about, and maybe someday there will be an answer as to how it all happened.

Be sure to take a long look at the elegant Adams-style fireplace mantel and the tile from Amsterdam titled "Jumping Jest." The mantel is original to the house and was created in 1820 by local craftsman Daniel Tolman. The finer homes in 1820 often had tile from Holland, as did Col. Ben and Lucy. The original tile disappeared, but we are so fortunate to have tile from Amsterdam that was created around 1820. Be sure to look at the unique playful jumping animals painted on the tiles.

Dining Room

Now please follow Henry across the foyer into the dining room. On the way, be sure to look at the lock and doorknob on the front door. They are authentic reproductions of 1820s hardware. Look at how small the doorknob is! People were a lot smaller in those days.

The dining room table is set with Lucy's Spode pattern "Blue Tower" china. The privy and the dump revealed a lot about the Stephenson dishes. There were pieces of at least six different sets of dishes found that can be attributed to the Stephenson family!

The crystal bowl on the mantel belonged to Col. Ben's mother, Mary. The family story is that she carried this bowl across the Allegheny Mountains on her way from Virginia to Tennessee. The Irish crystal bowl is a little lopsided, which just means it is old and handmade. Julie, a descendant of Col. Ben's sister Isabella, loaned this beautiful bowl to the Stephenson House.

Hey, see the candle box on the side table? You know that to stay healthy a mouse needs tallow, which is what candles are made of. So, the candle box was made so a mouse could not reach the candles inside. The Stephenson House mouse family did not like that box at all.

The Baltimore fancy chairs are really old and are the same kind as Col. Ben sold in his store here in Edwardsville. Ol' Henry thinks the tables are really clever because you can make two big tables for dining or each can be separated into two narrow tables. These narrow tables can be placed to the side so the dining room can open up for music and even dancing!

Master Bedroom

Let's go upstairs! Ol' Henry loves the large beautiful windows on either end of the stairs landing. Great-great grandpappy Ezra loved to spend time on this landing with the breeze coming through the open windows.

You all please follow Ol' Henry into the master bedroom to the south. This bedroom, with its beautifully carved mantel, was Col. Ben and Lucy's retreat from the servants, children, and the many people who stayed for extended visits. And in the old days, folks entertained guests in their bedroom. Lucy and her lady friends probably enjoyed tea at a table like the one currently in the room while they discussed Female Sunday School activities. In 1831, Lucy wrote a letter to a friend, and she may have written it in this very room! Lucy's letter, loaned to the House by Dotty, a great-great grandniece, will be displayed here when a safe way of preserving the letter is determined.

Isn't the elegantly carved mahogany bed with a canopy, curtains, and deep, soft featherbed absolutely wonderful? The probate records listed each piece of furniture in the room and also noted the bed was mahogany.

The portrait above the mantel is of Mary Reed Stephenson, Col. Ben's mother. This portrait is a copy of the original portrait that is now in extremely poor condition. Julie, a descendant of Isabella, Col. Ben's sister, loaned the portrait to the Stephenson House.

The original 1820s closet doors are painted and glazed the very color that Lucy chose, and we know this through a paint analysis of the millwork in the house. Just think, Lucy and Col. Ben used these very closets over 180 years ago!

Col. Ben and Lucy were married twenty-three years when he died here in this room. From Virginian legal records, it is known that in 1799 Lucy was ten and a half years old when she married thirty-year-old Benjamin Stephenson. Yes, that surprises most everyone! Henry learned that "Indian" Van Swearingen, Lucy's father, died when she was seven years old, and her mother soon remarried. It is speculation, but maybe that arrangement wasn't good for Lucy. It is not known what the marriage arrangement was and any guess is pure speculation. However, Lucy obviously received the education her father had provided for her in his will.

She was a loving, supportive wife and later became the mother of four children who adored their father. The marriage worked!

Children's Bedroom

The Stephensons had four children. The three younger children, James, Elvira, and Benjamin V., moved into this house with their parents. The oldest child, Julia, born in 1803, married Palemon H. Winchester the year before the move. Let's go across the hall into the children's bedroom.

This is really a super children's room. You can see there are two beds, one with a lace canopy and the other a trundle bed. The children who tour the house love this room because they are permitted to tighten the rope bed springs, play on the bed, and dress up in period clothing. Look at the toys, the cradle, and the copper bathtub. Just think how much hot water had to be brought from the kitchen to fill the tub for a bath. No wonder the early folks didn't take a bath every day!

The door I told you about earlier is on the west wall. It led to the servants' sleeping quarters above the attached kitchen where they were near to care for the children during the night. Ol' Henry loves this room. It just feels good! Can't you just see the Stephenson kids playing and sleeping here?

Well, that concludes Henry's tour of my favorite things in Col. Ben's house. I hope you enjoyed the tour and will come back and visit again. There is always something new and interesting to learn or see on each visit. Thank you for joining me on my tour.

See ya' later!

Henry

DESCENDANTS OF COLONEL BENJAMIN STEPHENSON

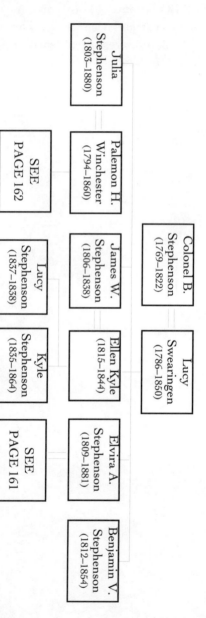

DESCENDANTS OF ELVIRA STEPHENSON

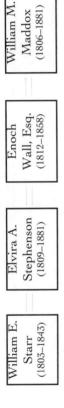

William E. Starr (1803–1843)

Elvira A. Stephenson (1809–1881)

Enoch Wall, Esq. (1812–1858)

William M. Maddox (1806–1881)

Male Starr (1828–1840)

James Starr (1830–1860)

William H. Starr (1832–1881)

Female Starr (1836–1880)

DESCENDANTS OF JULIA STEPHENSON

Julia Stephenson (1803–1880) — Palemon H. Winchester (1794–1860)

Children of Julia Stephenson and Palemon H. Winchester

- Lucy Ann Winchester (1821–1822)
- Marion S. Winchester (1823–1854)
- Sarah A. Winchester (1827–1854)
- Elvira A. Winchester (1828–1877)
- Ellen M. Winchester (1830–1865)
- Benjamin S. Winchester (1832–1899)
- Laura Winchester (1838–unknown)
- James A. Winchester (1842–1873)
- Texanna Winchester (1845–1847)

Marion S. Winchester (1823–1854) — Nicholas Boice (1810–1860)

Sarah A. Winchester (1827–1854) — Benjamin Brazzell (unknown)

Elvira A. Winchester (1828–1877) — Milton Sims Matthews (1816–1875)

Children:
- Julia Matthews (1851–1861)
- Lawrence Matthews (1853–1855)
- Marion E. Matthews (1855–1914) — George M. Dearing (1849–1888)
- Sarah V. Matthews (1857–1880)
- Fannie S. Matthews (1859–1872)
- Laura A. Matthews (1861–1933)
- Nicholas A. Matthews (1864–1947)
- Lucy S. Matthews (1866–1952)
- Milton S. Matthews (1868–1875)

Children of Marion E. Matthews and George M. Dearing:
- Fred Morris Dearing (1879–1963) — Dorothy Sittenham
- Milton M. Dearing (1881–1955) — Maud Helm (1879–1953)
- Frank W. Dearing (1884–1956) — Mary D. Suddoth (1888–)
- Charles G. Dearing (1888–1975) — Jeanette Thornton (1893–1970)

Children of Charles G. Dearing and Jeanette Thornton:
- Marie Thornton (1897–)
- Joseph S. Barr (1896–)
- David L. Thornton (1898–1966)
- Susan F. Jefferies (1905–1985)

Ellen M. Winchester (1830–1865) — William W. Freeman (1829–1900)

Children:
- Marion S. Freeman (1856–1914)
- William H. Freeman (1858–1914)
- Virginia W. Freeman (1859–1914) — David Laws Thornton (1829–1900)
- Edwin W. Freeman (1844–1923)
- Frank Freeman (1862–1880)

Benjamin S. Winchester (1832–1899) — Brookey A. Yowell (1840–1930)

STEPHENSON HOUSE MOUSE TRACKS

Great-great-great grandfather Samuel
Came from Virginia in 1809 with Benjamin and Lucy Stephenson,
tucked away in their household goods

Great-great grandfather Ezra
Ezra hid in a hat box in 1816 when he came from Kaskaskia to
Edwardsville with the Stephenson family

Great granddaddy Amos
Amos was raised at the Stephenson House and traveled in a bureau
drawer in 1834 when he accompanied Lucy to Carlinville, Illinois

Great uncle Thomas
Brother to great granddaddy Amos and remained at Ben and
Lucy's house when she went to Carlinville, Illinois

Henry
Long-time resident of the Stephenson House at 409 S. Buchanan
Street, Edwardsville, Illinois

STEPHENSON HOUSE MOUSE COUSINS WHO VISITED THE HOMEPLACE

Cousin Elijah – Lexington, Kentucky
Cousin Elzey – Columbia, Missouri
Cousin Jake – Lower Town, Edwardsville, Illinois
Cousin Maggie – Lexington, Kentucky
Cousin Seth – Carlinville, Illinois
Cousin Van – West Virginia
Cousin Zach – Kaskaskia, Illinois

Ancient Cousin Isaac – Columbia, Ohio
Isaac was the great-great-great grandson of granddaddy Josiah of
the Swearingen mouse family.
Josiah lived at Fort Swearingen, West Virginia, when Lucy
Swearingen Stephenson was born.